The Beloved Community

WRITTEN BY

WENDELL J. DAVIS, SR.

FOREWORD BY

DR. MARK WHITLOCK

The Beloved Community
by Wendell J. Davis, Sr.

Copyright © 2024 by Wendell J. Davis, Sr.
All rights reserved.
Printed and bound in the United States of America

Published by Cole Publishing

Originally published as "The Church as the Beloved Community: Providing for the Relevant needs of the Homeless," in fulfillment of the requirements for the degree of Doctor of Ministry for Payne Theological Seminary
Wilberforce, Ohio
August 2019

Chapter images from Unsplash.com.

No reproduction of any part of this format, contents or artistic contributions can be made without written permission from the author.
Library of Congress
Cataloging-in-Publication Data
ISBN: 979-8-9885825-4-0

Cole Publishing
4067 Hardwick Street #282
Lakewood, CA 90712
Email: ccpprod@aol.com

Book Cover Design by Covenant Images
Book Interior Design by DesignAnneli.com

For Book Orders: Contact us at Cole Publishing Company

Cole Publishing

CONTENTS

DEDICATION

I would like to dedicate this book to my biological mother Pinkie L. Street, grandmothers MaDear Pearlie Woodard & Sefronia Starks, high school head coach Taja Rodisha, junior school teacher Dr. Michael White, mentor Dr. Perry J. Jones, and over 25,000 clients I have been blessed to house in Trinity In His House Foundation Transitional Housing and Sober Living Homes. These individuals truly were my village, and they ALL played a major role in helping to shape my life and guide me in the direction that I have taken. For this reason, I do my very best to pay it forward by imparting to others what they have deposited into me. They have taught me how to be responsible and accountable, have integrity, fight and never give up, and be respectable, disciplined, and confident in myself and my abilities -along with working hard and laying everything I had on the line for success.

SPECIAL THANKS

A very special thanks to Dr. Candace Cole Kelly for encouraging and inspiring me to get this book out, providing me the platform to do so through her company Cole Publishing, and and walking every step in a methodical and amazing time frame. You and your outstanding expert team of professionals have assisted me with taking my dissertation and transforming it into a masterpiece of my journey, truly capturing Dr. King's Beloved Community. I would also like to thank Dr. Mark Whitlock, my mentor, who embraced me at a time when I was facing a defining moment in ministry and life. He helped to polish the rough edges off me and expand my ability to do business, secure business, develop my ASK, and master my plan. Dr. Whitlock helped me to go from average to establishing the rules for engagement, success and capital-raising, increasing my assets by using the Cecil Murray Plan which he helped to develop. I will be forever grateful to Mark, Dr. Cecil Murray, and the USC Center for Civic Engagement and Public Policy.

ACKNOWLEDGMENT

I would also like to acknowledge my father, Wardell Jerry Davis, who taught me how to be a man, and how to take care of my family. I will forever thank, love, cherish, and miss this man of God who believed in me so much that you could not tell him I was not the greatest preacher and son that ever existed. The love and pride that he showed me for my accomplishments in life before his death 18 years ago have only increased because he was only blessed to witness half, but my greatest honor in life was to be his son and his pastor. I shall forever be grateful and honored to carry his last name and DNA.

To my dear sweet wife, Trevina LadyT Davis, the apple of my eye and love of my life, I thank you for believing in me, trusting me, and rolling with a brother since 9 and 11 years old. Thank you for blessing me with two amazing children, my awesome son Wendell Jr. and my amazing daughter Wenikka Davis, and the joy of my life today, my grandchildren: my first love Lyric Amore Elcan Davis, my miracle baby Laylah Princess Elcan Davis, and my namesake and Paw Paw boy Legand Deuce Elcan Davis, whom I love with every ounce of blood in my veins and every breath of life.

My family is my greatest blessing, joy and success. I love them beyond infinity and pray that my children's children maintain my legacy, philanthropy, and gift to serve others. I dedicate this writing in honor of my twin grandson who rests in heaven with Jesus, Legend Elcan Davis.

Dr. J. Wendell Davis, Sr.

FOREWORD

Dr. Mark Whitlock

The Beloved Community reflects the lives of millions of Black men struggling to survive in urban communities. Bishop Dr. Wendell Davis's book caused me to reflect on my own life as a Black man and a father of three sons living in Los Angeles, California. As I read, my eyes began to leak tears of joy and pain, and my spirit was renewed to build the Beloved Community.

I believe most Black men can relate to not having a meaningful relationship with their fathers. Since 1970, seventy percent of Black fathers have not been actively involved in their children's lives. The truth is, it is not only the problem of absentee fathers that creates negative outcomes for Black children, but systemic problems that lead to violence, sexual abuse, inadequate schools, food deserts, and the lack of adequate health care.

Young people are called by God to create the Beloved Community, but the call from the streets seduces future pastors, professionals, and legitimate businesspeople to become members of street gangs, hustlers, pushers, and players. Children of Generation X and Y have experienced more bullying, mass shootings, police brutality, crack cocaine addictions, free online pornography, and teenage funerals than any other generation in the history of America.

I feel every pastor experiences a few key moments in their ministry journey, moments when they hear God inviting them to a higher calling. It is when we listen to God and obey Him that we come out of ourselves into God's greater purpose for our lives. Yet all too often white noise, social media reels, and foolish chatter cancels out the call of God. I remember so clearly in my ministry feeling like an imposter and unworthy of pastoral leadership. This book brings the clarity of God's call and purpose through acceptance of the calling of compassion for the least of these.

Through these words, Bishop Davis reminded me of the urgent need to mentor young people who feel like imposters, unworthy of God's calling, and living without knowing God's purpose. This book is not an option: we must follow in Bishop Davis's footsteps as he walks with Christ to do more than just preach and pray, but develop sports and mentoring programs, recruit coaches, and train men to become faithful fathers who are actively involved in their children's lives.

Dr. Davis said it well: "Pastoring is not limited to preaching." When Jesus said to His disciples, "Follow me and I will make you fishers of men," Jesus commanded us to bring the lost to Christ. Preaching is not intended to entertain the saved but to equip the saints to bring the lost to Christ. If you want to end gang violence, human trafficking, drug abuse, bullying, absentee fathers, and senseless deaths, read this book. **Memorize it. Reflect on your life. Absorb the principles**. I want to thank Bishop Wendell J. Davis, Sr. for coaching me when I felt like giving up on pastoral ministry. I am a better pastor today because he spoke God's word into my life. If *The Beloved Community* does for you only a part of what it did for me, your life will never be the same.

Dr. Mark E. Whitlock, Jr.
Pastor, Reid Temple AME Church, Glenn Dale, MD

INTRODUCTION

Communities all across America are in crisis. We are more untied than united, fragmented because of racism, sexism, classism, and the great political divide. We are in dire need of Shalom - or, as Martin Luther King Jr. called it, the Beloved Community.

I invite you to imagine a community where the whole needs of people are addressed - where, despite their brokenness, they can come to receive a hot meal full of dignity, or a gift card so they no longer have to choose between groceries or a roof over their heads. Imagine a community center that doubled as an after-school hangout for homeless youth, and a designated safe zone where their family could park their car (which they sleep in) for the night. Imagine a church where single parents are supported, those with addictions or a history of incarceration are welcomed, old wounds are healed, and broken families are made whole. Imagine a church that can proclaim the gospel without ever needing to use words. The Beloved Community will show you how this can be a reality.

For over forty-five years, I have been searching for this Beloved Community. From my beginnings as a young boy growing up in some of the most dangerous neighborhoods of Los Angeles, to God's call on my life to remain in this same city in full-time ministry, I have been working to put flesh to this vision, believing that the Church can - and must - be part of building a whole community. Through every setback and celebration of this journey, I have discovered more about myself and the ministry God had for me.

And I believe you can, too.

Perhaps you are like I was, struggling along as you see your small church dwindling. Do you feel, as I did, that it's two steps forward, one step back? Do you see mounting challenges in your surrounding community, and feel that the Church is missing its opportunity to engage?

We as the Church are the Body of Christ here on earth. We are involved in the condition of humanity, and have been created to address these holistic needs right where people live, work and worship. I believe that each church body, in its own way, is called to build the Beloved Community where God has placed them. And although each body is unique, I am here to tell you that there is a model you can follow. It takes trust and shared leadership - a willingness to know and be known by your particular community.

In this book, I would like to share with you the hard-won knowledge I have gained from many decades of this work and the extensive research I have done. In the chapters that follow, I will share more of my story with you, from a young boy sneaking down to the altar call one Sunday, through a dangerous life of gang involvement, to decades of pastoral calling and the struggling church of New Jericho Christian Church. We will explore the historical and biblical foundations of the Beloved Community, effective systems and models to follow, and case studies that examine what this looks like in action. I will even share specific resources for you to use, as well as suggestions for how you can contextualize this model in your community. By the end, I hope this book will not only inspire you, but show you the way you can build the Beloved Community right where you are.

THE CONTEXT THIS BOOK WAS BORN OUT OF

It is a true saying that we must know our community to serve our community. The context for this book is New Jericho Christian Church, located deep within the inner city of Los Angeles, California, where I have pastored for the past sixteen years. As we examine the building blocks of a Beloved Community, I will share research, case studies, and other resources with you that have their foundations in this specific church context, as well as suggestions to contextualize them wherever you are.

Trinity In His House is the non-profit arm of New Jericho Christian Church, started twenty years ago from nothing out of my frustration with the secular workforce. I wanted to do ministry full-time with enough flexibility to engage in various community projects. Trinity In His House promotes a simple yet profound vision of addressing the needs of individuals who reside in communities torn apart by economics, politics and prejudice. It provides shelter, counseling, and hope for homeless individuals to gain a better way of living than on the streets. In addition to this work, we have created a Child Development Center which focuses on after-school care and mentoring. These services were all born out of a knowledge of the needs of the community and a vision of the Beloved Community which continues to flourish to this day.

In essence, we looked around at our community and asked: How many children have been raised in single-parent homes? How many widows live in the community? How many grandparents are raising children for the second time? Are parents separated due to incarceration? Then, once we discovered the answer to these questions, we developed modalities to address those needs. We asked: what would happen if we invited church members into this space to use their various areas of expertise? What if we expanded the vision of what a church could be outside of Sunday morning? The result was a community flooded with new resources and on its way to fulfilling the vision of Dr. King as the Body of Christ.

Whether you're new to the idea of King's Beloved Community, have been working in the trenches of church ministry for a long time, or are seeing your church aging and dying and wondering what in the world you have done wrong, I pray this book will prove to you that the Beloved Community is possible - if only we take a chance and begin.

CHAPTER ONE

Out of Myself and Into the Greater Self of God

My journey to write this book began over fifty years ago. Although a variety of life experiences have been good, great, not-so-good and even chaotic at times, they have prepared me for pastoral ministry today. Because of them, I had to discover myself, leave myself, settle with myself, examine myself and even challenge myself through the years. I had to find the real me inside of me. I had to come out of myself into the greater self of God. If God in His sovereignty were to call me home today, I can truly say that it is well with my soul, I have fought a good fight, I have trusted Him where I could not trace Him at times and I have remained steadfast in my quest for His righteousness. As we begin our exploration of what it means to live in a Beloved Community, come walk with me as I take you on a journey of my own spiritual life.

A CHILD OF THE BAPTIST CHURCH

I was baptized in All Nations Missionary Baptist Church under the late pastor D. L. Spigner, at the age of seven. Before this, I attended the House of Prayer Holiness for the first seven years of my life, and that was a very traumatic experience of confusion, embarrassment, and discrimination. We worshiped Sweet Daddy Grace, A.K.A. Bishop McCollough, more than we worshiped God. I can remember staying up all night to receive a dollar bill from the Bishop during his visits. I can remember food cooking in the church to sell to the members to raise money. However, I could never figure out why the church would not feed the poor; which was me, my family and many members of the congregation. If you could not buy a meal, you definitely would not get anything to eat. I could not understand why the church would not allow me to eat, knowing that my mother was a drug addict and single parent.

I loved going to church to worship. I loved the instruments, shouting, testifying, dancing, singing, and miracles being performed. I loved the excitement when the Bishop would come to town. Still, I hated to see my family members go hungry and give every penny they had to the church and the Bishop, while living in the church hotel starving from a lack of food, working every day, broke, and hungry because the priority was the church and the Bishop.

Then Mrs. Katheryn took me to church with her one Sunday. The Sunday school maintained a student store after class where you could get sodas, chips, candy, or cookies; and if you did not have any money to purchase anything, they would give it to you. All Nations Missionary Baptist Church was refreshing for me. This church got my attention, it was a small caring church and the pastor helped the people. I liked this church, so I tried to join on the first visit, but Mrs. Katheryn would not allow me to join. She would pinch me or prevent me from joining the church. On one particular Sunday, I decided the next time Mrs. Katheryn tried to stop me, I would go between her legs and run down to the altar. As fate would have it, I made it to the altar and joined the church. Ultimately, my whole family joined and was baptized. We sang in the choir, worked in the church, and supported the ministries. Amazingly, this helped to change my mother's life. Who would have thought that a little child would be responsible for the entire family getting baptized and joining a church?

My moral box was formed by the Baptist church. The Baptist church taught me right from wrong, to confess my sins to God, pay my tithes, give offerings, feed the hungry, clothe the naked, and help your neighbor as though you were helping yourself. The church taught me to study the scripture for myself and trust the Holy Spirit for memory, conviction, and conversion. I enjoyed the fact that in the Baptist Training Union (BTU) there would be prizes and gifts for learning memory verses and publicly quoting scripture. Out of all the teaching and learning experiences I had, the Baptist church was the best biblical foundation and teaching institution I have ever attended.

The Baptist church taught me a sense of family. I was born out of wedlock; at that time, my mother was twenty-five years old from Ruston, Louisiana, and had three children. Her childhood sweetheart and husband brought her to California and abandoned her and his children, which forced her to live in her aunt's garage. My father was a country bumpkin in the big city; a slick player, gambler, and whoremonger from Baltimore, Maryland, whose mother died when he was nine years old. Once he encountered my mother and got her a place to stay, the rest was history.

Needless to say, I learned to do everything grownups did. By the time I was eight years old I was introduced to drugs; using it, selling it, cutting it, and even hiding it from my mother.

I was exposed to older girls and grown women who forced me to have sex with them. This occurred because my mother was always high. I remember trying to talk to her about her drug use, and she whipped me for talking about it. I learned never to mention anything to her again. I was grateful that no man touched me, although they tried. I was streetwise and talkative, causing them to believe I would tell. I was a child who spoke as if I was grown.

PREPARED FROM MY MOTHER'S WOMB

My mother used to tell me that she wished that she had flushed me down the toilet when I was born. I was a Black baby by this high yellow Creole woman that had three other children that were high yellow with green eyes, and here comes this chocolate baby that looks just like his whorish father.

God saved me from my mother and preserved me for such a time as now. It hurt me growing up with this type of spirit from my mother and then my siblings. My Cherokee Indian maternal grandmother in Ruston, Louisiana, would tell me where my big nose came from, my dark skin color, and my heritage: it was my Ma Dear who instilled in me that I was somebody.

Nearly 90% of the males in my community made it out in a body bag, police car, or Jesus Christ. I am grateful that God changed and saved me.

It was my grandmother who gave me the choice of words and the history of where the high yellow skin color came from. It was my grandmother who taught me to cook, clean, work, and take care of myself. I learned from Ma Dear how to live and to live well. I was delivered and did not understand the magnitude of my destiny and deliverance. My greatest ministry moments were for my grandmother to hear me preach in her church, tell me how proud she was, and be blessed to eulogize this giant of a mother who helped me learn how to live and survive insults.

MY FIRST FAILURE

My first failure occurred in the fourth grade. The neighborhood bully, whose name was Roger, took my candy and slapped me. I tried fighting him because I considered myself to be tough and age was just a number for me; Roger was seventeen years old. He shoved me off, and I left crying. I told my sixteen-year-old brother what Roger did, and since we lived in the hood, you could be punked by anyone.

My brother confronted Roger regarding taking my candy. Roger and my brother got into a fight which ended in Roger stabbing my brother and causing him to be hospitalized. This event took place one year after my stepfather was murdered on our front porch by our next-door neighbor. Through experiences like these, I became numb to violence, pain, and suffering.

One thing I can never forget: my school put me in special education classes simply because of my poor behavior. We had one class all day. In reality, I was not a candidate for special education; rather, I was hungry, tired, and lonely because of my environment. I was raised with violence and other crimes that surrounded me. I needed a good home, cooked meals, sleep without worrying about who may break into our home, and a mother who would not use dope at night.

Eventually, all of this led me to join a street gang. By the time I was in the sixth grade, I was assaulting grown men on public streets. The owner of a local store hired me and my cousin to keep us and other youngsters from stealing.

Although I was saved, I had three cousins locked up in a Northern California prison for murder. They killed one to two people within a square mile of our community. I understood why my mother's father would put his hands on my shoulders and call me Reverend. I always shrugged my shoulders and wiggled his hands away from me saying, "I am not going to be a preacher; I am going to be a gangster." My grandfather passed away when I was ten years old, and it was a blessing for my family. After this, we moved just four miles south of our neighborhood to a community that I thought was Beverly Hills by comparison. This turned out to save my life.

As I look back over my life, I can see God's hand over me. Nearly 90% of the males in my community made it out in a body bag, police car, or Jesus Christ. I am grateful that God changed and saved me.

In our new neighborhood, I went to a new school. People in that community could not handle me, because I had come from a gladiator community four miles north. When I entered Junior High School, a graphic arts teacher by the name of Michael White took a liking to me and my gang friend Reynaldo; this would change my life. I learned how to make business cards, printed envelopes, letterheads, stamp pads and custom cards on old press machines. I realized I could sell these things and make money: he got my attention, and everything shifted overnight.

Mr. White told me that I had to start passing my other classes if I wanted to remain in his print class — I was failing every subject except homeroom. He would have me come into his class during recess, lunch, and after school to tutor me. Soon, all my grades improved, allowing me to print again. One day, he took me on a walk-through Juvenile Hall, and I determined that day that I did not want to go to jail. Mr. White changed my thinking: although I was still banging on the side, I was a good athlete, a tough gangster, and becoming a good student. If it had not been for Mr. White, I would not be the man I am today. God indeed used him to help me when I needed it most.

SPORTS AND TEACHERS SAVED ME

I also played baseball, basketball, football, track and volleyball. You could not miss me because I was competitive and enjoyed battling for bragging rights, reputation, and dominance, just as I sought it in the gangs. I began to get really good at football and track, and people started noticing me.

Coaches wanted me to play on their teams, and that meant that they would pay for my registration and make sure that I got to the field and games. What hurt the most, was that my mother never saw me play sports; she never took the time to encourage me or attend. I never had a parent in the stand to cheer for me, but my two older brothers would be there threatening me and charging me to do everything right and be the best. Other children's parents were also cheering for me, because I was that player that made things happen.

I also wished my father would have seen me play sports more than he did. It was not until my senior year of high school that my father attended his first game of mine, and saw me play ball. He heard my name constantly called out over the loudspeaker; he was proud of me and I was proud that he made it to see me.

When you can trust God where you cannot trace Him, He will show up where you least expect Him.

Another event around this time changed the trajectory of my gang involvement, and ultimately my life. When my eldest brother was shot and almost killed in a hardware store in our community, it sent a red light off in my head. When I arrived at the hospital, my brother could not talk to me, but I got him to write about who shot him. I will never forget him writing that the man had a blue rag on his head and was a Crip, a member of my gang. This devastated me: the very people I was willing to ride or die with were trying to kill my brother. I promised God that night that if He would allow my brother to live, I would leave the gang and only do sports and work. I kept my promise and God was faithful to save my brother and me at the same time.

IT TAKES A VILLAGE

My father was self-employed all of my life. He owned a wrecking yard and I remember going to work as young as four years old, doing miscellaneous things in the wrecking yard. At sixteen, I was buying cars as scrap and getting excellent prices.

I would never exchange my lifestyle, even though my father never married my mother and she was one of his women. My father took me to his home with his wife and she treated me well. Even to this day I have an amazing relationship with her, and I thank God that my father taught me to not be like him, but better. Before my father died, he was a proud parent, best friend, member, and supporter of our church and my ministry. He constantly bragged about me, which caused grief with my siblings at times. This made me battle to survive and do well in life.

It was the same with my coach Bruce Hill, a childhood legend, a master-degreed college graduate, and a superstar in high school and college, discriminated against at the professional football level because he was Black and a quarterback in a time when whites did not allow it. I loved this guy for nagging, pushing, disciplining, and motivating me to go pro in life. He took time to plot a positive course in life for me, even though I was not the only athlete in the crowd. I did not understand it then, but now, I look over my life and see where God has brought me, how God has kept me, and how God used others to preserve me. I am grateful and understand that I never would have made it without God using a village to keep me.

As for my teachers who made a tremendous impact on my life, they became the parents I needed to keep me from developing a compromising, inferior disposition, or a poor distorted belief in myself. They encouraged me to believe that if I could dream it, think it, envision it, or write it down, I could achieve it. My coach taught me that if I made a play, even if it was not the right play, it would show him what I was thinking, and he could correct my moves and thought process. He taught me that I could not leave any man behind, to sell out on the football field, leaving it all on the line, and not to have any reservations or questions as to whether or not I tried or gave my best.

I walk through life today with the same athletic disciplines taught to me long ago. I bind them upon my head as frontlets, I recite them going in and coming out, and I have learned that when you give your all and your very best, you can live with your efforts and not have any remorse. However, I still had some struggles ahead before these lessons would fully integrate into my behavior and the new life ahead.

WORKING FOR THE WRONG REASONS

I realized every job I took prepared me for what God intended for me to do. I discovered I was making money, but for the wrong reasons. I made money to survive and party, but not to succeed and thrive. I had no plan or career goals. I had no advisors. I was self-centered and had difficulty perceiving reality. I was living in a make-believe world and my priorities were all messed up. I worked my first real job for the Los Angeles Unified School District (LAUSD) in high school as an assistant janitor and I had to go straight to work my senior year right after football practice. Upon graduation, I attempted college, but I was so broke and poor that I could not sit in class trying to learn on a hungry stomach. I was not qualified for financial aid and my mother was on welfare with two children at home; this crushed me.

BACK ON THE STREETS TO SURVIVE

I dropped out of school and started selling dope, and I was able to get a car, and clothes, and have money in my pocket. I remember going to my father and he told me that he could not help me through college, that hurt. However, as the dope game picked up, I was able to get another job with LAUSD as an adult, and I became a custodian within two months. Then I became permanent within my first year. Eventually, I was promoted to supervisor, known as a Plant Managers Assistant, then Plant I, then Plant II, and finally Plant III over four years. Unfortunately, staff began to harass me, and I lost my job, which created my first major crisis in my adult life.

This was particularly a crisis for me because I was married at nineteen, and at twenty-three years of age I had a wife and child. In need of money to support my family, I turned again to drugs. My mother-in-law told me that she heard that I was selling dope and I told her it was none of her business. She went on to say that I did not need to sell dope, but if I would just go back to church, pay my tithes and offerings, and give unto God, He would take care of me and give me anything that I could ever want or imagine. I do not need to tell you that I have a habit of listening to wise counsel, learning from other's experiences, taking constructive criticism, readjusting in the midst of adversity and following what I feel works. I tried what my mother-in-law advised, and today, God has blown my mind with favor, grace, covering, and mercy. When you can trust God where you cannot trace Him, He will show up where you least expect Him.

SAVED FOR SURE

I called my father and told him what I was experiencing, and he said I needed to pray and talk to his pastor. I went that Sunday to his church to talk to Pastor Hayes Reed at Greater True Light Missionary Baptist Church. The pastor stood me in front of the church, he laid hands on my forehead and all I felt was hot burning fire and the power of God. I knew then what I have known since I was seven years old and joined All Nations: that God had saved me and called me to not only preach but pastor.

Since then, I have been on fire for God in Jesus Christ. I started helping people find themselves. I have been favored by God, and if He does not do anything else for me, He has done enough already. I mean this to the core of my heart. I am eternally grateful to my Lord and Savior Jesus Christ.

PASTORING IS NOT LIMITED TO PREACHING!

I accepted my call at Olivet Institutional Baptist Church in Ontario, California. Pastor David Turner pressured me to preach my first sermon. I did not have the message yet and I was waiting on God, so three months went by until he told me that I could not sit in the pulpit until I preached and that I had to sit with the deacons. I did not care about that: I had been a deacon for years and taught and spoke several times. Finally, the Lord gave me the word and it was the Great Commission. I notified the pastor and he set the date, and everyone came from all over to support me as I stood to preach. I preached like thunder and lightning, causing Pastor Turner to get upset. Pastor Turner said, "This boy has been preaching for years," and each pastor in attendance agreed. After that trial sermon, I preached every Sunday for two months while the pastor went on vacation.

While on vacation, members of the congregation tried to make me the pastor. I told them that I would tell Pastor Turner about it, and when I told him he laughed at me. To make a long story short, they put him out later on. But on the third month of my trial sermon, my father's pastor died and I was called to pastor my first church at twenty-nine years old. I do not need to tell you that my entire family left the church with me.

As I look back over my life and ministry, I can see that God has always been there for me, even when I could not be there for myself. I discovered that my life preaches my sermon. I thank God that my life speaks for itself; as bad as things may have been, they could have been worse, and I thank God for helping me through. Because of my past experiences, I have been blessed to organize substance abuse ministries to treat people for what my mother did not have the opportunity to get treated for. I have established transitional facilities that provide housing and a clean and safe environment for single mothers with children returning from prison. As a ministry, we have organized child development centers to provide an excellent early childhood education for children, and a counseling school to prepare clergy and parishioners to minister to the hurting and wounded. From the fruit of this work, we organized and planted a new church ten years ago, and were able to purchase three properties, including the ideal property we wanted for ministry. Families have been renewed, restored, and revived through our ministries, children have been reunited with their parents, and men's transitional facilities assist returning addicts and felons in rehabilitating back into society, employable and equipped. In all these ways, we specialize in holistic healing and deliverance.

| CHAPTER TWO |

Seeking a New Model

Charles Marsh once wrote, "The beloved community may be described as a gift of the kingdom of God introduced into history by the church, and thus exists within the provenance of Christ's mystery in the world."[1] The Beloved Community consists of integrated worship, social service agencies, youth programs, and civic engagement initiatives that operate within the church. Martin Luther King said, "The church and the community as *the Beloved Community* is an affirmation of who we are as well as a clarion call to better ourselves, our community, our city, the nation and the world."

Simply put, New Jericho Christian Church is on a mission to create the Beloved Community. The Black church needs a new model for ministry: the historic focus of Black churches on worship and Bible Study growth. Previous lenses are now too narrow - they do not sufficiently address the evolving and expanding needs for spiritual development, nurturing youth and families, or providing social services for both church members and the larger community. Neither does the historic focus of churches to track their good works, change church culture, or establish fiscal transparency; each of which is essential. The traditional model also lacks the structure to support the needs of the new church. All of these factors have convinced New Jericho that the current model needs re-thinking, reinventing, and re-tooling. In response, we began what I now call the Beloved Community Project, aiming to expose the challenges faced by churches limited by tradition and describe new methods of becoming the Beloved Community we all desire. The goal was to develop a model for churches, especially small ones, to better serve the community where people live, work, and worship.

---

1   Charles Marsh, *The Beloved Community: How Faith Shapes Social Justice from the Civil Rights Movement to Today* (New York, NY: Basic Books, 2005), 207.

THE CHURCH BIRTHED OUT OF PROBLEMS

New Jericho was itself organized through a mission to become the Beloved Community, but you may be surprised to learn the history of New Jericho was birthed out of church problems. As a senior pastor for twelve years, I had to step down from a ministry in which I merged two churches. Our coming together created a membership of over 500 members and dual responsibility for both pastors to assume the responsibilities of pastoral and administrative duties.

I was fully aware that my gifting in ministry was in leadership and administration. I can preach with minimal effort because I have always been a talker, someone who could persuade others to follow. I have also always led by example, whether it was good or bad. However, I have not always been one who could pick out a bad apple with strong discernment. Of course, this has come back to haunt me in various situations when trouble and disappointment have risen in ministry.

I started pastoring at the age of twenty-nine, and after four years at my first church, a historic Baptist church in the city recruited me to be their pastor. I was subsequently voted in by a unanimous vote of the congregation. The church was known for being a "hellish" church that had had over nineteen pastors in a thirty-nine-year span, with the longest-tenured pastor making it two years. I accepted the pastoral position for several reasons, one of which was that it paid well, considering my first church only paid me twenty-five dollars per week sometimes. Second to this was the motivation of pastoring a church that had two hundred members, as well as the fact that it was a historic church, and the church that exposed me to BTU. Despite their track record, I became the longest-tenured pastor at the McKinley Avenue Baptist Church in thirty-nine years.

The Lord provided protection and kept me from dangers seen and unseen. He has a way of getting your attention and having you do what He called you to do. Two months after of our church merger, He called me to birth New Jericho Christian Church ministries. In fact, He had given it before I left McKinley Avenue Church, but I ignored God and did what others wanted, rather than what I knew God had told me. I learned my lesson, and never again will I delay paying attention to the Holy Spirit.

We organized New Jericho Christian Church Ministries in December 2007 with fifteen people in a member's home the Sunday before Christmas. It was amazing, frightening, and enlightening. We also received confirmation as the ministry grew to 174 members, and we never looked back.

New Jericho purchased a building in our first year of ministry, after much prayer and God's divine power. Three months later, another bank gave us a church three miles from our first church. We rented it out to two other churches, and two years later the Lord led us to purchase a third sanctuary where we currently worship for a fraction of the cost.

It was at the Cecil Murray Center for Civic, Public Policy & Social Justice at the Dornsife School of the University of Southern California that I learned about contractual negotiations, nonprofit organizations, and policy changes. My tenure under Dr. Murray and Pastor Whitlock changed my life, ministry, finances, business, church, and future. New Jericho went from eight employees to twenty-one, and grew from $1.2 million in assets to over $6 Million, from an annual revenue of $375K to $2 Million. We were able to grow and stabilize our ministry, nonprofit, church and business health. We were also able to stabilize and limit our debt. It could only be the Sovereign God we serve who orchestrated this amazing, once-in-a-lifetime opportunity.

I knew we had to do something quickly if our church was going to survive the major crisis of that season.

Since then, our ministry has been able to give birth to nine new churches, and assist other ministries around the country with resolving church conflict and negotiations of new loans or saving their properties from foreclosure.

As I look back on where my life began, I remember promising God that if He would deliver me from the hell I was in, I would open the doors that He blessed us with to be a witness of His grace and mercy in ministry. He has certainly held up his end of the promise.

MINISTRY WHILE THE CHURCH IS DYING

The current context of ministry is frightening. It is frightening because as I was creating the Beloved Community with my nonprofit ministry, Trinity In His House Foundation, my church was dying. Yet Blacks, whites, Latinos, and Asians were living together in the same home, working together, getting clean from drugs and alcohol addictions, staying out of prison, and getting their own permanent housing for the first time in their life.

We managed to provide housing over the past seventeen years for over five thousand families, employment services for hundreds of felons, permanent housing for hundreds of people, deterred hundreds from returning to prison and established multiple facilities throughout Los Angeles County, all while our church continued to die. Our attendance dropped between twenty-nine to fifty-three members weekly. Although our offerings had gone up, we experienced a great reduction in membership for four years, and were not able to build back up. We had managed to grow a few new members through mentoring men and women, and public leadership in membership organizations; however, we did not have a team in the church that could commit or dedicate themselves to growing the church ministry. I sensed no sense of urgency to do better.

As a pastor, burnout was fast approaching. It started with my preaching and agitation with ministry. I bargained with God to change my current situation and bless me with a new ministry and people who had a mind to work in building God's kingdom. I lost my motivation to keep reinventing the wheel and building up, only to have dissenters come in and tear down. Although I trusted in God and continued to have hope, I did not feel I had the help, encouragement, support, or laborers with the same level of faith.

I knew our community crisis needed to be addressed educationally, considering the high rate of high school dropouts and citizens without a GED (see data below). I saw other needs in the community, such as family-based programs to address single-parent households, childhood nutritional programs, counseling for families, single-parent counseling, and married couples counseling.

Seeing these needs, I challenged myself to conduct strategic planning sessions with church members, ministry leaders and staff. I decided these sessions would include reviewing the church's vision, mission, and values in addition to defining the church's community and future demographics. The primary goal of the strategic planning session would be to grow our current membership by 50%.

I knew we had to do something quickly if our church was going to survive the major crisis of that season, in order to retain what we had and increase as we strove to grow beyond the walls of our church and become a church that looked like the Beloved Community. I believed we could do it; however, I also discovered in that season that I needed a break, a sabbatical, to rest, plan, renew my strength and get better prepared to make a run for greatness as we sought to rebuild the ministry and reach out to our community for the first time with a fresh start.

KNOWING YOUR COMMUNITY

You have to know your community to serve your community. In our work to build the Beloved Community here in our neighborhood of Los Angeles, California, we realized that we needed to know the demographics of our neighborhood, in order to serve them better. What we discovered has transformed our ministry, our church, and therefore our community, creating opportunities that strategically meet the specific, tangible needs of our neighbors and introduce many of them to the church for the first time.

The following pages contain examples of the kind of demographic information we researched in order to get to know our community better. I encourage you to do the same as you examine ways to build the Beloved Community where you are.

RACE

%	ETHNICITY
69.9%	Black
31.9	Latino
18.7	White
2	Asian
.4	Native America
18.7%	White Alone
31.9	Hispanic or Latino
2	Asian Alone
60.0	Black or African American Alone
.04	American Indian & Native Alaskan

MEDIAN HOUSEHOLD INCOME
IN NEW JERICHO SURROUNDING COMMUNITY

INCOME	ZIP CODE AREA
41,449	90043
43,494	90302
66,114	90305
74,959	90056
51,538	Los Angeles
86,571	View Park-Windsor Hills
57,952	Los Angeles County
36,134	90008
40,913	90047
37,293	90062

AVERAGE HOUSEHOLD INCOME

INCOME	ZIP CODE AREA
66,113	90043
57,866	90302
84,836	90305
112,969	90056
82,042	Los Angeles
112,047	View Park-Windsor Hills
85,514	Los Angeles County
59,215	90008
55,335	90047
49,048	90062

PER-CAPITA INCOME

INCOME	ZIP CODE AREA
26,687	90043
21,499	90302
33,016	90305
47,886	90056
29,878	Los Angeles
46,015	View Park-Windsor Hills
29,301	Los Angeles County
28,316	90008
20,815	90047
15,316	90062

HIGH INCOME HOUSEHOLDS

%	ZIP CODE AREA
5.1	90043
1.5	90302
5	90305
13	90056
7.5	Los Angeles
13.5	View Park-Windsor Hills
7.6	Los Angeles County
2.7	90008
1.9	90047
.8	90062

MEDIAN HOUSEHOLD INCOME BY AGE OF HOUSEHOLDER

MEDIAN HOUSEHOLD INCOME	90043	LA	VIEW PARK	LA COUNTY
Householder under 25 years	22,281	26,745	0	29,622
Householder 25 to 44 years	40,184	54,558	101,570	60,520
Householder 45 to 64 years	48,408	58,469	103,233	67,426
Householder 65 years and over	36,900	38,383	65,500	42,310

RELATIVE INDUSTRY CIVILIAN
EMPLOYMENT POPULATION 90043

%	INDUSTRY
6.72	Transportation
19.2	Healthcare
12.2	Education
6.3	Government
1.02	Utilities
3.44	Education
5.8	Administrative
6.37	Other Services
10.3	Retail
2.17	Entertainment
3.42	Finance & Industry
5.89	Hospitality
4.2	Construction
1.42	Real Estate
5.22	Manufacturing
1.25	Wholesales
.52	Agriculture
1.7	Oil & Gas
.06	Management

EMPLOYED MALE AND FEMALE

%	INDUSTRY
0.0 – 0.1	Armed Forces
49.5 – 52.8	Employed
7.7 – 13.3	Unemployed
42.8 – 33.8	Other
60	Between 16 - 65

EMPLOYMENT AMONG THE MARRIED

%	CLASSIFICATION
31.2	Both parents work
10.5	Stay at home moms
.8%	Stay at home dads
1.8	Neither parent works
25.3	Both wo
6.5	Ladies who lunch
7.9	Gents who lunch
17.7	Neither work

EMPLOYMENT AMONG THE MARRIED WITH CHILDREN

%	CLASSIFICATION
70.1	Both parents work
23.5	Stay at home moms
1.8	Stay at home dads
4.2	Neither parent works

EMPLOYMENT AMONG THE MARRIED WITHOUT CHILDREN

%	CLASSIFICATION
45.5	Both parents work
11.8	Girls who lunch
14.2	Gents who lunch
28.2	Neither Work

EMPLOYMENT BY EDUCATIONAL ATTAINMENT

%	EDUCATIONAL ATTAINMENT
77.5	Bachelor's Degree
64.6	Some College
61.3	High School Diploma
57.5	No High School Diploma

NON-WORKING BY RACE FEMALE & MALE

%	ETHNICITY
51.7 – 64.1	Mixed
40.4 – 44.5	Black
44.6 – 33.4	Hispanic
41.1 – 35.3	Other
38.2 – 22.0	White
36.9 – 13 5	Asian

UNEMPLOYMENT BY RACE FEMALE & MALE

%	ETHNICITY
22.4 – 22.1	Mixed
20.1 – 13.0	Asian
10.2 – 19.5	Other
8.8 – 15.4	Black
7.9 – 12.8	Hispanic
5.2 – 2.3	White

CHAPTER THREE

A Connected Community

The King Center describes the Beloved Community this way: "Dr. King's Beloved Community is a global vision in which all people can share in the wealth of the earth. In the Beloved Community, poverty, hunger and homelessness will not be tolerated because international standards of human decency will not allow it. Racism and all forms of discrimination, bigotry and prejudice will be replaced by an all-inclusive spirit of sisterhood and brotherhood."

When I began casting a vision for this new project, I knew it needed to expose the challenges that churches face when they are limited by tradition and describe new methods of becoming the Beloved Community. My goal was to develop a model for small and medium-sized churches to better serve the community where people live, work, and worship. I believed that the answer to many of our struggling churches today was to rise up and establish the Beloved Community.

Charles Marsh wrote, "The beloved community may be described as a gift of the kingdom of God introduced into history by the church, and thus exists within the provenance of Christ's mystery in the world." The Beloved Community is an integrated house of worship, social services agency, youth programming center, and civic engagement initiatives think tank that operates within the church. As Martin Luther King Jr, said, "The church and the community as the Beloved Community is an affirmation of who we are as well as a clarion call to better ourselves, our community, our city, the nation and the world."

The context of New Jericho Christian Church was perfect for developing this project. It had a dying membership, but a young, educated congregation living in the largest percentage of African American communities in Southern California: Lambert Park. This area suffers from racism by police officers, a 57.5% high school dropout rate, homelessness, crime, education, marriage and family issues, and poverty.

I believed the church needed a revolution: a dramatic change from doing business as usual. Therefore, we decided this project would require the resources of the church and Trinity In His House to develop programs, provide resources, and create activities that had a measurable social impact in Los Angeles, California. Trinity focused on real estate development, educational training, parenting programs, homeless housing, reentry services, social justice and community development initiatives. These programs were created and managed by both paid and volunteer staff. We looked to merge Trinity's work efforts and resources along with New Jericho Church to provide programs, create budgets, and socially impact the church and community toward Trinity's many services. We knew this merger could also be used to help build ministry through services offered in the community.

Young people today do not feel their voices are heard, alienating them from the more mature members of the church.

At the time, New Jericho Church had seventy people on the church membership roll and an average of thirty-five people attending for Sunday worship. The church had purged its membership roll two years before this project began and removed the names of members who had not come within six months and contributed financially. This gave us a true sense of who we were as a church. We determined that we needed to grow; however, we were not sure how to make it happen. I could see that this ministry project would become the blueprint to refocus our ministry geared around providing the desperately needed services of our church and community.

New Jericho confronted multiple pastoral care challenges as well. The church had to sustain a minimum of $2,000 of income per week, at a time when the Christian movement seemed to be growing smaller. Demographically, people are not attending church as in the past. Each time I conduct a funeral of a senior member who contributed financially and was very committed to the ministry, we never recover from their loss. To cultivate commitment of this caliber takes years of teaching and training, and it seems that churchgoers young and old are no longer interested in serving God or their local church as a high priority.

In order to do what was necessary for New Jericho church in this millennial era, we needed workers, brilliant minds, and interested individuals who wanted to make a difference in their community and the world. Yet each time I gained one, I lost one. Each time I took two steps forward, I lost three steps backward.

Our church needed to conduct a community needs assessment to reveal ways to meet the needs of the congregation and community. I believed that if we held various sessions with leadership and the church geared around the church's vision, mission, and values, and determined where we needed to launch and land ministries, we could become more effective. In this way we would have a better understanding of the spiritual, social, and physical needs of church attendees.

As we assessed our current congregation, we saw several overarching themes across three age group demographics in the community surrounding New Jericho: youth, young adults, and adults.

Theme 1: Creating A Connectional Community. The idea of the "Church family" should permeate the church while impacting the community. Churchgoers wanted a greater connection to the family—to be known and to know others—through events beyond church services that are sponsored by or held at the church. Regardless of age and stage, the community wanted to see the church provide broader participation in the community.

Theme 2: Youth & Children Programs. We needed to address both the adult groups and youth groups (ages 13-18) because our ministry needed high-quality youth programs and services. Our conversation needed to be centered on including social activities not only on Sundays but also during the week. In general, our church needed to do more to encourage and embrace youth creativity and passion for social justice. Young people today do not feel their voices are heard, alienating them from the more mature members of the church. We learned we could make a difference by simply providing snacks and food during services, since our church was situated in a community where 91% of the public education students received the Federal Subsidized school lunch program.

Theme 3: Information Sharing & Communication. Communication has been a concern with adults in our church. Members expressed dissatisfaction with how information is disseminated throughout the church. Diversifying how information is communicated was a key factor in member's attendance and participation.

Theme 4: Consistency. New Jericho can often be inconsistent in the way it functions, leaving members uncertain about what they can plan or expect. For example, we do not tend to start on time or end services on time consistently. We have leaders who will cancel a program because they failed to do the work in informing everyone of the services and their need for support in the program. Members fail to return to afternoon services when they are scheduled. We have tried Bible study several times and have experienced poor attendance. Through this assessment, we learned our Christian education would be better served if we had committed leaders to assist with the delivery of these services and not rely solely on the pastor.

Theme 5: Ministries. Because of limited resources within New Jericho, we needed to determine a set core of ministries that we could deliver and remain consistent in our delivery through financial support and volunteerism. We needed to determine how to integrate these ministries/services for more effective impact and results and establish our church as a viable institution in our community.

Theme 6: Bible Study. We needed to reestablish a Bible study that connected with the sermon for Sunday morning worship. We determined that we could select specific topics and Bible verses for each Sunday session, and introduce and teach that topic to all groups (children, high school, young adults, adults and seniors). This provided adults and family members with the opportunity to continue discussions at home and model those behaviors and values that are important to one's spirituality.

Theme 7: New Jericho Family Activities. New Jericho had done well for over ten years as a church and accomplished a tremendous amount of success in this short period of time. Yet, we had lost significant members who were vital to the sustainability of our ministry. We needed to develop our congregation to spend time as a cohesive unit, build relationships, and empower members. We needed to encourage church leaders to consider new approaches to church activities/events where all members participated. The intent of family activities was to:

- Promote a high level of cooperation between all members

- Build and maintain effective interpersonal relationships

- Encourage open discussion of ideas, opinions and suggestions

- Identify champions for new projects or programs.

New Jericho needed youth and young adults in order to survive, and we needed to engage our youth participation in the overall activities of the ministries. We knew we could do this by having ministries such as youth movie nights, fun nights, open forums, family nights, and karaoke. For youth and young adults to remain active, the church needed to teach and provide a sense of community, belonging, urgency and discipline. Young people stay in the church when they are drawn into the community by faith and socialized into a community that affects their actions, beliefs, attitudes, values, and even their dating habits.

The synergy between my spiritual background and the church ministry context became a strong partnership for renewal, revival and revolution. After all, the post-modern church is not the church of my grandparents. The post-modern church needs a revolution. The post-modern church lacks resources, the millennial generation is missing, the internet has members' podcasting sermons on cell phones, and church activities are failing to meet the needs of the congregation. We are living in perilous times. Churches are needed for us to rise up to end racism, unseat immoral politicians, speak truth to power to crooked police, develop jobs, help the homeless, end gun violence, establish training programs for youth, and lead sinners to Christ. I knew we could accomplish the goal of creating the Beloved Community by following a proven model. Together, we moved forward in this effort to reimagine the "Church as the Beloved Community."

CHAPTER FOUR

How to Walk the Walk

Since the Beloved Community was given popularity by Dr. Martin Luther King, Jr., it has come to be defined as a society based on justice, equal opportunity, and love of one's fellow human beings. Diametrically opposed to the notion of a Beloved Community is the ongoing race war and power struggle aimed at keeping races and communities separate at all costs. This race war, which has moved from being a covert operation to becoming very public in recent years, is one of the defining reasons our country has the plethora of social ills we are experiencing today.

Yet despite these social ills, the Beloved Community is a path forward toward a more civil society where a sense of equality and justice prevails. Therefore, it is important to learn from those who are grappling with solutions to bring harmony in communities, especially in multi-cultural and multi-ethnic communities and where "white flight" is slowing to a halt.

EVERY COMMUNITY HAS ITS STRENGTHS

The basic premise behind community organizing is creating a community of people who are there when you need them and when they need you. Community organizations come in many shapes, sizes and varieties; however, they have at least two values in common:

1. They strive to develop as sense of community among their members.

2. They organize people to do what they cannot do themselves.

In a world where problems and power (or the lack thereof) exist, community organizations are a method of getting things done and solving problems that affect you. They can realign the balance of power by bringing people together and grouping those with like concerns. In this sense, the church can be viewed as a community organization.[2]

To be effective in community organizing requires people to be aware of their own self-interest while building relationships with others and channeling their desire to change the community and/or the world. It takes "understanding how groups work, why people join them, how to pay for them, how to set dues, goals, and rules, how to develop values, and how to move people to action. Successful groups need solid internal management, good group process, secure funding, effective communication, and a sense of trust and community among their members."[3]

According to Brown, Americans have held to two beliefs about individualism and community. On the one hand, Americans believe in and glorify the self-made man; yet on the other hand, they relish a sense of community where people are neighbors who help each other out. Institutions or the state or federal government cannot solve many of the problems found in communities. It is in these cases that communities of people are galvanized around a common interest, believing that the problems they face can be solved.[4]

It is important to remember that in order to solve problems and improve the situations people face, the active participation of the people most affected by the problem(s) is required. Alfred J. Marrow summarizes this notion best by saying,

> A man who joins a group is significantly changed thereby. His relations with his fellow members alter both him and them. A highly attractive group can bring great pressure to bear upon its members; a weak group will not have as much molding power. The whole is different from the sum of its parts; it has definite properties of its own.[5]

Whether the organization is a congregation, a neighborhood civic association, a community group, etc., many of the group dynamics required to build a strong organization are the same. All organizations require strong group development to be

---

2   Michael Jacoby Brown, *Building Powerful Community Organizations* (Arlington, MA: Long Haul Press, 2006), 1.

3   Brown, *Building Powerful Community Organizations*, 3-4.

4   Brown, *Building Powerful Community Organizations*, 8

5   Brown, *Building Powerful Community Organizations*, 8.

purposeful and successful. Organizations are always looking for ways to build community, ways for people to know each other better, and ways for people to come into face-to-face contact with each other. When people are placed together who share a common interest, even if it is just four or five individuals, they can come up with a powerful action plan to improve their situation.[6]

Because of this, Brown recommends the following steps when building a successful community organization:

1. Start with an idea

2. Develop the vision

3. Start with yourself; what makes you tick

4. Listen to others

5. Put your organization in writing

6. Develop a sponsoring committee

7. Bring the core group together

8. Take action and execute the visionary plan.[7]

When these eight steps have been executed with precision and passion, the result over time will be a well-intentioned and powerful organization able to act on issues that are of significant importance to those who make up the group.

A CREATIVE APPROACH

Unlike Brown's approach to community organizing, Si Kahn's approach uses what he calls the "creative approach" to organizing. With this approach, Kahn moves beyond the traditional methods to strategically get things done, especially when seemingly insurmountable obstacles stand in the way (such as legal and political systems). According to Kahn in his book, *Creative Community Organizing: A*

---

6   Brown, *Building Powerful Community Organizations*, 15.
7   Brown, *Building Powerful Community Organizations*, 16.

Guide for Rabble Rousers, Activists, & Quiet Lovers of Justice, there are twenty steps to taking action toward solving the problems of community involvement. These twenty steps are paraphrased and summarized below:

1. Most people are motivated primarily by self-interest. This becomes the glue that binds the people together toward a common purpose.

2. Institutions and people who hold power over others rarely are as united as they appear on the surface. The goal is to get these institutions and people to stay out of the fight.

3. Begin the process by imagining the step just before victory and work backward to develop the steps to get there.

4. Take a positive stand or position and then oppose the negative position.

5. The greater the task, the more difficult it will be to accomplish. In this case, ask the participants to do one thing and one thing only.

6. Regardless of how divided people may be, if the cause is right, they will always find a way to rally around it. Therefore, leave the stereotypes at the door.

7. People are always partly united and partly divided. Your goal is to rally the people around the unifying causes as you work with them.

8. Demonstrations are still effective. You must find less confrontational ways of being seen and heard.

9. Make sure that all participants are clearly aware of the risks and losses they may suffer both individually and collectively before acting.

10. Work hard at asking questions that will cause participants to think deeply about the answers.

11. Be cheerful in the face of adversity and help others feel that way.

12. The more you are sure of yourself in a particular situation, the more you must work to avoid imposing your personal feelings on others.

13. Hold institutions to their goals and responsibilities. At worst, form another organization to force the original institution to do its job or to replace it.

14. When people who have not had power get it, there is no guarantee that they will exercise it any better than those who had it before.

15. There is no guarantee that people will be able to see beyond their own situation. Work on being transformational for the cause of the mission rather than being instrumental.

16. The thought that organizers are violent people is not true. It is a tactic to discredit the organization from being victorious.

17. You should not only go with what you know but with who you know. Relationships are critical. Make sure you give people options for how they can serve and get involved.

18. It is easy to shift from representing a community as its spokesperson to being its leader, even when you don't live in the community.

19. It is never certain what people can accomplish together; therefore, never compromise with injustice.

20. The beloved community is not just a futuristic goal; it is something that can be experienced every day while working toward the ultimate goal. Celebrate the small victories along the way.[8]

By following these twenty creative organizing steps, organizations will have a greater opportunity to move the barriers that plague people and give them the power to act in ways that transform their personal and communal concerns. The more successful organizational actions become, the greater the ability of the organization to gain more members and create more power to act in the face of opposition.

Sandhya Rani Jha believes that there are two primary strategies for transforming communities: strength-based strategies and asset-based community development. In her book, *Transforming Communities: How People Like You Heal their Neighborhoods,* Jha provides timely resources for community leaders to get a handle on how to live and lead faithfully in an increasingly polarized world, ravaged

---

8   Si Kahn, *Creative Community Organizing: A Guide for Rabble Rousers, Activists, & Quiet Lovers of Justice* (San Francisco, CA: Bernett-Koehler Publishers, Inc. 2010), 193-196.

and torn apart by racism, sexism, xenophobia, economic disparity, and political isolation.[9]

A strength-based approach to care, support and inclusion looks at what people do with their skills and their resources, and what the people around them can do in their relationships and communities. People need to be seen as more than just their care needs—they need to be experts and in charge of their own lives. The critical attributes of the strength-based approach to care are:

- The individual's personal resources, abilities, skills, knowledge and potential

- Their social network and its resources, abilities and skills

- Community resources, also known as social capital and or universal resources

Jha suggests that because so much work with marginalized communities comes from a space of charity, or "us serving them," it sometimes misses a key element that solidarity brings: a "me journeying with you" alternative framework. By contrast, a charity model pays attention to the needs of a client and sometimes unintentionally or unconsciously focuses on his/her limitations or failings. Neighborhoods that have seen a lot of disinvestment (wealthier people leaving, diminished city funding, departure of local business, decreased taxpayer-funded maintenance of public space) are often told what others will do for their neighborhood as if their role is solely to be recipients. Even if their input is sought for the neighborhood development process, often their input is not sought regarding what their neighborhood should look like.[10]

In these uncertain times, churches and our broader society must make a sincere commitment to engaging in acts of compassion and justice as a means of living out our faith and loving our neighbors.

---

9   Sandhya Rani Jha, *Transforming Communities: How People Like You Are Healing Their Neighborhoods*, Atlanta, GA: Challis Press, 2017), 2.
10   Jha, *Transforming Communities*, 12.

Asset-based community development begins by looking at what gifts exist within a neighborhood. Here are a few basic keys to helping any neighborhood be its best:

- Use an asset lens: look for strengths in the community

- Be inclusive: recognize potential leadership in unexpected places and foster it

- Evaluate your assets: inventory the strengths you find, in ways that build trust among community members

- Be action-oriented: move straight from assessment to tangible improvement efforts

- Let the community direct the spending (as opposed to developers or city staff).[11]

By incorporating either strength-based or asset-based development, we can bring trust, cohesiveness, and a willingness to work with outside resources for the betterment of the community.

In *Creating the Beloved Community: A Handbook for Spiritual Leadership*, Jim Lockard explains that the Beloved Community is created when people commit to a spiritual pathway to seek a closer relationship with God, and when people take their spiritual awareness into the world to be examples of love and compassion in action. Lockard says that the Beloved Community is about being truly dedicated to walking your talk—to being in full alignment with spiritual principles.[12]

The Beloved Community's core mission is to reveal and to heal—to honestly confront issues and to compassionately make corrections as they unfold. Lockard believes that today, this challenge must be undertaken among people who live in evolving cultures with shifting value systems. Through spiritual leadership, Lockard believes that community leaders can explore together some of the external and internal obstacles to creating the Beloved Community, as well as how to overcome them.

---

11   Jha, *Transforming Communities,* 12.
12   Jim Lockard, *Creating the Beloved Community: A Handbook for Spiritual Leadership* (n.p. Jim Lockard, 2017), 1.

Ultimately, these obstacles can be overcome through evolving leadership, providing a safe space to grow together and express possible differences, and taking action that will bring the community together in solidarity.[13]

CARING FOR EACH OTHER

Another way to build the Beloved Community, according to Donald M. Chinula, is by providing pastoral care to the oppressed and underserved in the community. In his book, *Building King's Beloved Community: Foundations for Pastoral Care and Counseling with the Oppressed*, Chinula argues that care can become problematic, because the pathogenic institutional structures hurt persons on a wholesale scale, while clergy and other counselors, teachers and therapists struggle to help them find healing and wholeness on an individual scale. On the other hand, Chinula sees that King's pastoral-prophetic passion was to help bring God's healing power to the shriveled self-esteem, fractured identity, and feelings of ontological nothingness suffered by wounded victims of racial, ethnic, economic, and social oppression.[14]

According to Chinula, counseling is the process of providing assistance to distressed persons or groups of people in order to overcome the symptoms of their diseases and achieve wellness or healing. As a rule, counseling is employed when the distressing factor is believed to be predominantly emotional and psychological in nature.[15]

In preparing the reader to understand this side of community work, Chinula takes the time to define terms that are critical to providing care. The first word that is described is pastoral care. While the word "pastoral" may imply the individual providing the care should be ordained or a member of the clergy, the vocation of pastoral care and counseling is not limited to church officers. A wide array of persons who are educated, trained, and experienced in the integration of theological and psychological disciplines are also among those on the front lines of caregiving when the need arises in the community.[16]

---

13   Lockard, *Creating the Beloved Community*, 9.
14   Donald M. Chinula, *Building King's Beloved Community: Foundations for Pastoral Care and Counseling with the Oppressed* (Eugene, OR: Pilgrim Press, 1997), x.
15   Chinula, *Building King's Beloved Community*, xi.
16   Chinula, *Building King's Beloved Community*, xi.

Chinula defines oppression as the state or condition of being involuntarily dominated or controlled by another individual or group. Domination in this case is never consensual. Oppression can be multilevel and multifaceted, encompassing all aspects of the social order and resulting in deep psychological, emotional, and spiritual problems for those affected. When it comes to community, oppression is inclusive of its traditional forms, such as race, gender, and class; however, it is also inclusive of people who do not participate fully in the wielding of societal power in all its aspects or symbols.[17]

Identity is defined by Chinula as a person's sense of something called self, and an understanding of who one is in relation to that self and to significant others. It also includes one's perception of one's place in the created order, including a belief in a supreme power as creator and governor of all creation. It encompasses a felt sense that this supreme power is experienced in ways significantly similar to others like oneself and dissimilar to those unlike oneself.[18]

By contrast, Chinula defines powerlessness as the actual or apparent inability of a person or group of persons to achieve their desired goals due to obstacles in their path. Actual powerlessness is an objective measure of the inability present in the situation to realize goal achievement. Empowerment is the motive force to overcome powerlessness in all the discussed senses. The motive force can spring from the subject group or from an external agency. Empowerment can be socio-politically, economically, or spiritually grounded.[19]

The last term defined by Chinula is praxis, or practice. This word means the pursuit of a vocation, as in the practice of ministry or medicine. Praxis is a doctrine of liberation theology that teaches that liberation takes place only when the practitioner self-consciously becomes an agent of change, and acts to transform and to be transformed by the reality acted upon.[20]

According to Chinula, while there are a number of issues that present themselves in a community, one that is often neglected is care. When care is infused into

---

17   Chinula, *Building King's Beloved Community*, xi.
18   Chinula, *Building King's Beloved Community*, xi.
19   Chinula, *Building King's Beloved Community*, xxi.
20   Chinula, *Building King's Beloved Community*, xxi.

the fabric of community restoration, a sense of holistic wellness can emerge, making it possible for the sustainability of effort to take place.

Tony Hunt says, "We can continue to pursue Dr. King's vision of the Beloved Community by making a sincere commitment to community-building and social engagement." Hunt goes on to quote Dr King, who also said, "Everyone could be great because everyone could serve." In these uncertain times, churches and our broader society must make a sincere commitment to engaging in acts of compassion and justice as a means of living out our faith and loving our neighbors. Individuals, churches, groups, organizations, institutions and even governments can continue to pursue Dr. King's vision of the Beloved Community by making a sincere commitment to community-building and social engagement.[21]

Below are ten ways the Beloved Community can be established:

1. Support and develop community-wide plans aimed at expanding economic opportunities for racial-ethnic persons and women, specifically in the areas of housing, banking, and employment practices.

2. Actively participate in programs that reach out to help those in the most need — the hungry, the homeless, and the unemployed.

3. Do your part to assure that every inner-city and rural young person can look forward to an adequate education. Adopt an inner-city or rural school. Offer your skills where appropriate.

4. Encourage schools, colleges, and universities in your area to include the teachings of Dr. King and other freedom fighters in their curricula and programs.

5. Take specific actions to deal with the problems of drugs, alcohol dependency, teenage pregnancy, and family violence in your community.

6. Advocate for the removal of all weapons from our streets, homes, and schools. Support causes that promote freedom, justice, and peace abroad.

---

21   Tony Hunt, "10 Ways to Build the Beloved Community," *Lewis Center For Church Leadership: Leading Ideas,* January 11, 2017, accessed January 2, 2019, https://www.church leadership .com/leading-ideas/ten-ways-build-beloved-community/.

7. Help extend human rights, dignity, health, and economic well-being to all persons.

8. Actively oppose groups that promote hatred and violence. Vigilantly oppose racism, homophobia, xenophobia, and other forms of hatred in our communities.

9. Sponsor and participate in programs that encourage interracial, inter-cultural, and inter-religious goodwill and unity.

10. Read the Social Principles of your denomination and strive to make them an integral part of your life and the life of your church and community.[22]

BUILDING THE KINGDOM

Jeff Ritterman is the author of the powerful article, "Building the Beloved Community: Jesus, Josiah Royce, and Martin Luther King Jr.'s Prescription for a Healthy Society." Once proper accolades and tributes are extended to the Martin Luther King Center and the work of Dr. Martin Luther King, Jr., Ritterman gets to the heart of what he wants his audience to know. As a Catholic, Ritterman says that looking back, the vision of the "Beloved Community" is in many ways a secularized version of what Jesus called the "Kingdom of God." Too often Jesus is confused with the White Queen from *Alice in Wonderland*. Christianity, however, is not about "believing six impossible things before breakfast"; rather, following the way of Jesus is about practicing radical kindness and compassion in our day, just as Jesus did in his time and place—a love that dares to transgress cultural and tribal divisions.[23]

From that perspective, I think G. K. Chesterton's view on Christianity applies equally to Dr. King's vision of the Beloved Community: "[it] has not been tried and found wanting; it has been found difficult and not tried." Recall that for Dr. King, the Beloved Community was a "realistic, achievable goal that could be

---

22   Hunt, "10 Ways to Build the Beloved Community."

23   Jeff Ritterman, "Building the Beloved Community: Jesus, Josiah Royce, and Martin Luther King Jr.'s Prescription for a Healthy Society," Global Catholic Climate Movement, September 10, 2017, accessed January 3, 2019, https://catholicclimatemovement.global/building-the-beloved-community-martin-luther-king-jr-s-prescription-for-a-healthy-society/.

attained by a critical mass of people committed to and trained in the philosophy and methods of nonviolence." Given the effectiveness we have seen of the practice of nonviolence in the movements led by King, Gandhi, and others, what would it mean to work toward having "a critical mass of people committed to and trained in the philosophy and methods of nonviolence"? What might it look like if we reallocated even 1% of our nation's significant military budget toward teaching nonviolent activism? And then 2% the next year? Then 3% and so on?[24]

Ritterman goes on to say that according to the writing of King, the three greatest threats to building the Beloved Community are racism, materialism, and militarism. Ritterman raises the question, "In our own lives, what would it look like to seek to communicate with one another—even when we are stressed out—with less harshness and more with nonviolent compassion?" Reflecting on his life as a child, Ritterman says that attending youth camp was like an almost perfect, idyllic Beloved Community. "And I would sometimes think that we should just have the whole world live in summer camp all the time. As I got older, I began to see that the summer was an exhausting sprint for the adults—that while exhilarating, it was not sustainable year-round."[25]

If we see but do not seek change, then we talk the talk but do not walk the walk.

As a child, Ritterman envied the lives of the owners of the camp, who lived on the campgrounds year-round imagining it as a great way to live. However, as he got older and was drawn into the inner circle of the camping circle, he began to see that even the phenomenal camp directors and owners, who did so much to create the magic of camp each summer, were human beings like the rest of us with imperfections and rivalries. For the most part during the off-season, they lived not in the Beloved Community, but instead retreated to their respective homes and families.[26] This revelation gave rise to the notion that our world is not a utopian reality,

24 Ritterman, "Building the Beloved Community."
25 Ritterman, "Building the Beloved Community."
26 Ritterman, "Building the Beloved Community."

but it does give those who thirst after the Kingdom of God and the Beloved Community something to work and press our way toward.

Dr. Arthuree Wright of the United Methodist Church writes a compelling article providing twenty-five traits of the Beloved Community. Rather than espouse these steps individually, Wright makes the point that the Beloved Community according to Dr. King was not a present future, but rather a current reality that was and is attainable for those who seek to live in love and harmony with their neighbor (remembering the biblical understanding of a neighbor).

The twenty-five traits he identifies are:

1. Offers radical hospitality to everyone; an inclusive family rather than an exclusive club

2. Recognizes and honors the image of God in every human being

3. Exhibits personal authenticity, true respect, and validation of others

4. Exhibits recognition and affirmation, not eradication, of differences

5. Listens emotionally (i.e., with the heart) – fosters empathy and compassion for others

6. Tolerates ambiguity—realizes that sometimes a clear-cut answer is not readily available

7. Builds increasing levels of trust and works to avoid fear of difference and others

8. Acknowledges limitations, lack of knowledge, or understanding—and seeks to learn

9. Acknowledges conflict or pain in order to work on difficult issues

10. Speaks truth in love, always considering ways to be compassionate with one another

11. Avoids physical aggression and verbal abuse

12. Resolves conflict peacefully, without violence, recognizing that peacefully does not always mean comfort for everybody

13. Releases resentment and bitterness through self-purification (i.e., avoidance of internal violence through spiritual, physical, and psychological care)

14. Focuses energy on removing evil forces (unjust systems), not destroying persons

15. Exhibits unyielding persistence and unwavering commitment to justice

16. Achieves friendship and understanding through negotiation, compromise, or consensus – considering each circumstance to discern which will be most helpful

17. Righteously opposes and takes direct action against poverty, hunger, and homelessness

18. Advocates thoroughgoing, extensive neighborhood revitalization without displacement (this also applies to the Church – working toward responsible and equitable growth, discipleship, and worship)

19. Blends faith and action to generate a commitment to defeating injustice (not forgetting that injustice can also be found *within* the Church)

20. Encourages and embraces artistic expressions of faith from diverse perspectives

21. Fosters dynamic and active spirituality – recognizes that we serve a dynamic God who is not left behind by a changing world or people, and that a passive approach will not work

22. Gathers together regularly for table fellowship, and meets the needs of everyone in the community

23. Relies on scripture reading, prayer, and corporate worship for inner strength

24. Promotes human rights and works to create a non-racist society

25. Shares power and acknowledges the inescapable network of mutuality among the human family.[27]

The next step, according to Wright, is to use these resources to engage in exercises that help you in living into the Beloved Community.

In *Plantation Jesus: Race, Faith, and a New Way Forward*, Skot Welch and Rick Wilson say that Plantation Jesus is the twenty-first century way that people deny the pain of someone else's past or present in order to be comfortable with the suffering of others. Plantation Jesus is a god who is comfortable with pain and suffering, an idol who can only exist in oppression and codified bigotry. It has been around since Colonial America and provides faith-based justification for racism.[28]

The irony of Plantation Jesus is that those who espouse such a position of "getting over it," and "putting our past behind us," do not realize that it is hard to overcome precisely because America is a nation built on white supremacy. No matter our race or ethnicity, it is very difficult for any of us to see the whole picture, because we are living within a system that by its very nature is designed to make us ignore or overlook the inequalities and injustices built into its bedrock.[29]

Welch and Wilson believe that the first steps to healing the effects of Plantation Jesus are learning, seeing, and understanding. If we do not take what we have learned, seen, and understood to then seek after change, we are nothing more than noisy gongs and sounding cymbals. If we see but do not seek change, then we talk the talk but do not walk the walk. If we truly want to disavow Plantation Jesus and eradicate its forces within our society and the communities we live in, we must adopt the following practices of dialogue and communication:

- Recognize that these conversations are difficult but that everyone comes with the best intentions for the work

- Acknowledge when we have been hurt by something said by saying a simple "Ouch"

---

27   Ritterman, "Building the Beloved Community."

28   Skot Welch and Rick Wilson, *Plantation Jesus: Race, Faith, and a New Way Forward* (Harrison, VA: Harrison Press, 2018) 15-16.

29   Welch and Wilson, *Plantation Jesus*, 18.

- When someone expresses hurt, the conversation pauses to let the person who was hurt explain and the person who has caused the harm to hear and respond

- Give grace to everyone involved, including ourselves, without allowing space for racism and prejudice in the conversation.[30]

The Beloved Community is not a utopia, but it is possible. In the following chapter, we will continue to explore foundations of the Beloved Community by examining biblical truths as our guide.

---

30   Welch and Wilson, *Plantation Jesus,* 154.

CHAPTER FIVE

The Body, the Kingdom, and the Covenant

The New Jericho Community Church is on a mission to establish the Beloved Community in a local and global sense. New Jericho believes the traditional and historical methods deployed by the Black church in meeting the relevant needs of its members and people in the surrounding community are no longer effective. Therefore, to provide a progressive and fresh methodology to meet the needs of a dynamic church and community, which now serves a multiethnic congregation, we believe in establishing the Beloved Community as a local model of what can be, and then seeking to have it replicated by other churches in other parts of the city and country, as the best path forward.

The Bible has a lot to say about building a Beloved Community. To this end, it is important for us to now take a deep dive into some scriptures that will give us a solid foundation for this work. Join me on a journey through the Old and New Testament, as we look at the Year of Jubilee found in Leviticus 25, followed by the Body of Christ in 1 Corinthians 12.

The Year of Jubilee shows us that if we are to be the Beloved Community, we must take care to provide a season of relief and canceling of debts in addition to redemption and forgiveness. Leviticus demonstrates God's plan of redemption and serves as a reminder not only for the Israelites who were once in bondage, but for us today who have been freed by the power of the resurrection of Jesus from the dead. Freedom from economic, racial, social, and other forms of oppression allows people to live in love, peace, and harmony, which is the hallmark of God's plan of Jubilee.

The Body of Christ is a principle established by Jesus to usher in the Kingdom of God in the midst of God's people. The New Testament chapter of 1 Corinthians 12 shows us that because of the atoning sacrifice of Jesus on the cross, all people should live in harmony with one another since their sins have been forgiven. The Great Commission becomes the impetus for building God's kingdom on earth. Implicit in being the Body of Christ is the notion that we cannot live separate and apart from Christ, since Christ died for all people. The Beloved Community provides a critical understanding of what it means to live as the Body of Christ while establishing the Kingdom of God in our lifetime.

THE PROMISE OF JUBILEE

You shall count off seven weeks of years, seven times seven years, so that the period of seven weeks of years gives forty-nine years. Then you shall have the trumpet sounded loud; on the tenth day of the seventh month—on the day of atonement—you shall have the trumpet sounded throughout all your land. And you shall hallow the fiftieth year and you shall proclaim liberty throughout the land to all its inhabitants. It shall be a jubilee for you: you shall return, every one of you, to your property and every one of you to your family. That fiftieth year shall be a jubilee for you: you shall not sow, or reap the aftergrowth, or harvest the unpruned vines. For it is a jubilee; it shall be holy to you: you shall eat only what the field itself produces. In this year of jubilee, you shall return, every one of you, to your property. When you make a sale to your neighbor or buy from your neighbor, you shall not cheat one another. When you buy from your neighbor, you shall pay only for the number of years since the jubilee; the seller shall charge you only for the remaining crop years. If the years are more, you shall increase the price, and if the years are fewer, you shall diminish the price; for it is a certain number of harvests that are being sold to you. You shall not cheat one another, but you shall fear your God; for I am the Lord your God.[31]

LEVITICUS 25:8-18

Before we explore the Old Testament text of Leviticus 25 as it relates to Jubilee, it is important to establish a working knowledge of how Jubilee will be used in the text. First, there is a difference between the Year of Jubilee and the Book of Jubilees. The book of Jubilees is an important post-biblical Jewish writing telling the story of Israel's origins and paralleling the narrative flow in Genesis and Exodus. Having been given a revelation at Sinai, Moses is instructed to "write it in a book,"

---

31   Leviticus 25: 8-18 New Revised Standard Version of the Bible. Unless otherwise indicated, all scripture references in this document will be from the NRSV.

the same task assigned later to the angel of presence; in each case its revelatory value is assured. Jubilees' relation to the first two books of the Torah is so close that it has been designated as a "rewritten Bible," a literary work that presents and adapts a biblical narrative tradition to address issues and problems important to the writer's community.[32]

The author writes an adapted version of the stories of creation, the patriarchs (and matriarchs, especially Rebekah, more prominent here than in Genesis), and Moses' activity in Egypt, including his leadership in a covenant with God and revelation of the Torah. Jubilees expands the biblical narrative in several ways, often including rationales for Israel's festivals and laws in the days prior to their official origin or the revelation at Sinai.[33]

Completely separate from the Book of Jubilees, the Year of Jubilee is the biblical term for the fiftieth year in a series of seven Sabbatical Years. The Year of Jubilee (from Heb. yōḇel, "ram's horn") is the last layer in the extension of the Sabbath principle that begins with the day of rest every seventh day, extended in the Sabbatical Year (fallow every

> *Without being in a right relationship with God, it is difficult at best to be in relationship with one another.*

seventh year), to the Jubilee. It begins in the middle of the seventh sabbatical year (every 49th year) on the tenth day of the seventh month (the Day of Atonement), and extends, presumably, into the seventh month of the fiftieth year, thus overlapping by just over half a year with the regular Sabbatical Year.[34] The Jubilee Year, like the Sabbatical Year, was also to be a year of "rest" for the land, in which sowing, reaping, and harvesting were prohibited. The redemption price of land or slaves was to be pro-rated according to the number of years left until the next Jubilee.[35]

---

32   John C. S. J. Endres, s.v. "Jubilees, Book of," ed. David Noel Freedman, Allen C. Myers, and Astrid B. Beck, *Eerdmans Dictionary of the Bible* (Grand Rapids, MI: W.B. Eerdmans, 2000), 743.

33   Endres, "Jubilees, Book of," 743.

34   Robin J. DeWitt Knauth, s.v. "Jubilee, Year of," ed. David Noel Freedman, Allen C. Myers, and Astrid B. Beck, *Eerdmans Dictionary of the Bible* (Grand Rapids, MI: W.B. Eerdmans, 2000), 743.

35   Knauth, "Jubilee, Year of," 743.

God's Purpose for His People

Leviticus cannot be understood apart from God's purpose for His covenant people. In the account of Moses' struggle with Pharaoh in Exodus 4–12, God repeatedly called for the freedom of Israel to worship Him (4:23; 7:16; 8:1; 9:1; 10:3; 12:31). In a real sense the Exodus deliverance was incomplete until Israel began the worship of God at Sinai (Ex 3:12), thus fulfilling God's goal for the exodus. Israel was set free from Egyptian slavery and brought into a new covenant relationship with God precisely so that they might be free to worship.[36]

Secondly, Leviticus cannot be understood apart from God's desire to be with His covenant people. Since a Holy God cannot excuse the sin of his people, Israel's experiment in idolatry with the golden calf (Ex 32) presented God with a dilemma. Twice God warned the Israelites: "You are a stiff-necked people. If I were to go with you even for a moment, I might destroy you" (Ex 33:5; also see 33:3). How could a holy God continue to go with a disobedient and rebellious people? Exodus 34–40 and the Book of Leviticus answer that question by instituting commands and laws that the Israelites must live by.[37]

The overall burden of Leviticus was to communicate the awesome holiness of Israel's God and to outline the means by which the people could have access to Him. This is in line with the great central covenant theme of the Pentateuch, a theme that describes the relationship between the Lord and Israel. Just as a servant had to follow proper protocol to approach the king, so Israel had to recognize their own unworthiness to enter the sacred precincts of God's dwelling place. The gulf between the people and their God could be bridged only by their confession of their unworthiness and their heartfelt adherence to the rites and ceremonies prescribed by God as a precondition to fellowship.[38]

In order for the people of God to enjoy the benefits of being in relationship and fellowship with Him, holiness laws and standards had to be established. Without holiness laws, the people would not be able to access the presence or blessings

---

36   David S. Dockery, ed., *Holman Bible Handbook* (Nashville, TN: Holman Bible Publishers, 1992), 151.

37   Dockery, *Holman Bible Handbook,* 151.

38   Dockery, *Holman Bible Handbook,* 151.

of God. This is a critical understanding for the church in the twenty-first century; without being in a right relationship with God, it is difficult at best to be in relationship with one another. In order to establish the Beloved Community, the people of God and the community must understand how God has redeemed and saved them through grace and faith in Jesus Christ. When the Israelites observed the commands of God and walked in God's ways, things would go well for them. This sentiment must exist in the church and community today in order to receive the promised blessings of God.

The focus in chapters 25 and 26 of Leviticus is on Israel within their land. In fact, the word "land" is used thirty-nine times in these two chapters. The Lord's statement in verse 2 ("When you enter the land I am going to give you," NIV) must have been a great encouragement to Moses, especially after Israel failed to claim their inheritance at Kadesh-Barnea and had to wander in the wilderness (Nm. 13–14). If the Israelites were to possess and enjoy their land, they had to recognize and respect some basic facts, the first of which was that God owned the land (Lev. 25:2, 23, 38) and had every right to dispose of it as He saw fit.[39]

God also owned the people of Israel (v. 55), because He had redeemed them from Egyptian bondage. Because they belonged to Him, all the Jews were to treat one another as brothers and sisters (vv. 25, 35–38) and not take advantage of one another when it came to personal debts or property claims. The Jews were expected to toil in their fields, but it was God who gave the increase (v. 21) and supplied them with sunshine, rain, and harvests. In other words, the people of Israel had God as their "land Lord" and had to live by faith in His Word. This meant obeying His commandments and trusting His promises.[40]

Another important fact emerges from this chapter: God was in control of the calendar. God not only gave His people their land and their food, but He also gave them special times to observe so that the land would not be ravaged and spoiled. God is concerned about ecology and the way we treat His creation. Like

---

39   Warren W. Wiersbe, *Be Holy*, "Be" Commentary Series (Wheaton, IL: Victor Books, 1996), 121.

40   Wiersbe, *Be Holy*, 121.

the ancient Jews, we today are but stewards of God's gifts; we must be careful not to abuse or waste them.

Had Israel obeyed these principles, their economic system would have functioned smoothly, the land would have provided all they needed, and everybody would have been cared for adequately. However, they did not obey the Lord. The result was that the rich got richer, the poor got poorer, and the land was ruined.[41]

A Covenant for Success

The Bible is full of diverse and different literary forms. These literary forms serve to articulate the human experience from a divine perspective; they seek to share God's relationship with His people in a variety of forms, including figurative language, narrative history, poetry, wisdom literature, prophetic literature, gospel, oratory, and epistle. With the exception of a few passages, a significant portion of the Leviticus narrative is steeped with legal material of a cultic or ceremonial nature. The legal material is primarily presented in poetic form, with the exception of Leviticus 17–26, where Holiness Codes are described that befit the setting and context of God's plan to prepare His people to receive Him and enjoy His bounteous blessings and benefits.[42]

The legal form of most of Leviticus (primarily through prescriptions and statutes) suggests that it is part of a covenant text. In fact, it deals with the covenant requirements that regulate the means by which the nation and individual Israelites could enter into and maintain a proper relationship with the Lord God. In this sense Leviticus, like much of Exodus, is a body of covenant stipulations designed to help close the gap between God's holiness and humanity's sin.[43]

The covenant requirements in the book of Leviticus are as follows:

- The need for sacrifice

- The need for priestly mediators

---

41   Wiersbe, *Be Holy*, 121.
42   Dockery, *Holman Bible Handbook*, 151.
43   Dockery, *Holman Bible Handbook*, 151.

- The need for separation between clean and unclean

- The need for a day of atonement

- The need for holy living

- The blessing and curse

- Offering and dedication[44]

These covenant requirements instituted by God would ensure the Israelites' success as they prepared to enter the Land of Promise.

You Were Once Slaves in Egypt

The first thing that God commanded was for the Israelites to keep the year of Jubilee. After seven Sabbaths every seven years—that is to say, forty-nine years—the trumpet of Jubilee should sound through the whole land on the tenth of the seventh month, i.e., the day of atonement, to proclaim the entrance of the year of Jubilee. This mode of announcement was closely connected with the idea of the year itself. The blowing of trumpets, or blast of the far-sounding horn (*shophar*, see at Lev. 23:24), was the signal of the descent of the Lord upon Sinai, to raise Israel to be His people, to receive them into His covenant, to unite them to Himself, and bless them through His covenant of grace (Ex. 19:13, 16, 19; 20:18).[45]

Personal holiness must be carried out on the social plane on behalf of the dis-advantaged.

Just as the people were to come up to the mountain at the sounding of the ram's horn, or the voice of the *shophar*, to commemorate their union with the Lord, so at the expiration of the seventh sabbatical year the trumpet blast was to announce to the covenant nation the gracious presence of its God, and the coming of the year

---

44   Dockery, *Holman Bible Handbook,* 151.

45   Carl Friedrich Keil and Franz Delitzsch, *Commentary on the Old Testament*, vol. 1 (Peabody, MA: Hendrickson, 1996), 626.

which was to bring "liberty throughout the land to all that dwelt therein" (v. 10). This would include deliverance from bondage (vv. 40ff.), return to their property and family (vv. 10, 13), and release from the bitter labor of cultivating the land (vv. 11, 12).[46]

This year of grace was proclaimed and began with the day of atonement of every seventh sabbatical year, to show that it was only with the full forgiveness of sins that the blessed liberty of the children of God could begin. This grand year of grace was to return after seven times seven years; i.e. every fiftieth year was to be sanctified as a year of Jubilee. By this regulation of the time, in the view held by R. Jehuda and the chronologists and antiquarians who have followed him, celebrating the Jubilee on the forty-ninth year is proved to be at variance with the text, and the fiftieth year is shown to be the year of rest, in which the sabbatical idea attained its fullest realization and reached its earthly temporal close.[47]

On this High Holy Day, when reconciliation with God was to become a national petition, the Israelites were required to be properly restored to their brothers. Personal holiness must be carried out on the social plane on behalf of the disadvantaged. All Jews who for any reason had become enslaved to another Jew or were forced to sell personal property to someone in the preceding forty-nine-year period were automatically emancipated, and sold property was restored to its original owner.[48]

Slave laws in Exodus (Ex. 21:2–6) and Deuteronomy (Dt. 5:12–18) provide the option for a slave to remain with his master after six years of enslavement by agreement; yet in the Jubilee even that slave is set free. The restoration of sold properties to the rightful owners indicated that the land of Canaan was ultimately God's land (Ex 15:13, 17), and He could do with it as He wished. The restoration of the land to its original owner was also a protection for the weak; for the rich to dominate over the weak would be a violation of God's covenant. As in the sabbatical year (25:4–5), the Israelites were not to sow seed or gather crops during the Year of Jubilee (25:11).

---

46   Keil and Delitzsch, *Commentary on the Old Testament*, 626.
47   Keil and Delitzsch, *Commentary on the Old Testament*, 626.
48   Mark F. Rooker, *Leviticus*, vol. 3A, The New American Commentary (Nashville, TN: Broadman & Holman Publishers, 2000), 303–304.

Also, as in the sabbatical year, the people could eat only what was taken from the fields. This year followed immediately after the seventh sabbatical year, which meant that the land lay fallow in the seventh sabbatical year as well as in the following Year of Jubilee. Two fallow years in succession would have been a severe test of faith. The Israelites were called upon to trust totally in God and acknowledge in a profound way that He was the provider of their basic necessities.[49]

Israel's care for the poor and the stranger was based on the fact that the whole nation was once rescued from slavery by God (25:35–55). Israelites who became poor were to be lent money without being charged interest and were to be sold food at cost price. This enabled them and their families to continue to live in the same community. Israelites were never to become slaves to other Israelites. If they were forced to become servants, then they were to be released at the Jubilee. Foreigners and immigrants could be bought by Israelites as slaves. There was no law that such slaves must be released at the Jubilee. They and their children were the property of their Israelite owners and could be handed on to the next generation.[50]

God Will Provide

God required the Israelites to submit their will to His will so that He could bless them. To this end, many of the commands given by God might have appeared arbitrary or unnecessary. Yet this is because no one fully knows or understands the ways of God; not even the Jews. We see as much wisdom and goodness displayed in the commands we do not understand as in those in which we do.[51]

The command to give rest to the land every seventh year, when the extent of the country was so disproportionate to its population, must have appeared exceedingly strange to those who had not duly considered it. The generality of persons would account for it perhaps by being conducive to the good of the land, which would be too exhausted if not permitted occasionally to lie fallow. But this could not be the only reason: for then a seventh part of the land would most probably

---

49   Rooker, *Leviticus*, 303–304.

50   Andrew Knowles, *The Bible Guide*, 1st Augsburg books ed. (Minneapolis, MN: Augsburg, 2001), 79.

51   Charles Simeon, *Horace Homileticae: Genesis to Leviticus*, vol. 1 (London, UK: Samuel Holdsworth, 1836), 674–675.

have been kept fallow every year, and not the whole at once. Moreover, it would not have needed to produce anything, which would tend to counteract the main design; whereas all the seed that had been accidentally scattered on it during the harvest was allowed to grow up to maturity. Nor can the idea of lying fallow be applied with any propriety to the olive yards and vineyards, which, though not trimmed and pruned that year, brought all their fruit to maturity. We must then look to some other source for the reasons for this appointment.[52]

There are a number of possibilities as to why God required the land to rest during the seventh year. The most reasonable is seen in the discussion of verses 18–22, on the issue of how one might survive during the sabbatical year when one could not sow his crops. The answer to this question and other considerations is this: God will provide. God requires obedience, and if the people comply, they need not worry about what they will eat in the sabbatical year. The Lord will sustain and provide for them so that they live securely (25:18–19). If the Israelites are faithful, God will send such a blessing in the sixth year of the cycle that the land will yield enough food for three years. The yield would be so great that it would continue until two years after the sabbatical year (25:21–22). This promise of God's abundant blessing of food for which the Israelites do not toil is reminiscent of the provision of manna for the Sabbath day (Ex 16).[53]

Acknowledging that ultimately God owns the land should have motivated the Israelites to refrain from cultivating the land in obedience to God. Taking a year off from work in the sabbatical year and two successive years when the Year of Jubilee followed the seventh sabbatical year would force the Israelites to reflect upon the Lord as provider of all. The provision of crops did not depend on man's labor but upon God as the sustainer. Work is relative, for if needs are to be met in life, God must provide.[54]

We can read about the various seasons of Jubilee throughout the Bible and find encouragement, hope, and resolve to press our way when times seem uncertain and difficult. The Old Testament book of Leviticus and the Year of Jubilee gives an

---

52   Simeon, *Horace Homileticae: Genesis to Leviticus* 674–675.

53   Mark F. Rooker, *Leviticus*, vol. 3A, The New American Commentary (Nashville, TN: Broadman & Holman Publishers, 2000), 304–30

54   Rooker, *Leviticus*, vol. 3A, 304–305.

excellent example in the construction and development of the Beloved Community. Looking closely at the requirements of God shows that when we are obedient to the will of God, He will provide. It also tells us that whatever we do as humans is actually secondary to God's will. Often God must demonstrate His sovereignty in the face of human limitations before we understand how God provides. A Beloved Community is one where everyone is a follower of Jesus Christ and a believer in the commands of God. When we follow Jesus and believe in the commands and laws established by God, things will go well with us in the land that God will provide as the Beloved Community.

The next biblical text, 1 Corinthians 12, will explore how the development of the Body of Christ will contribute to the mission of New Jericho Community Church in establishing the Beloved Community for its local area.

THE BODY AND THE KINGDOM

> For just as the body is one and has many members, and all the members of the body, though many, are one body, so it is with Christ. For in the one Spirit we were all baptized into one body— Jews or Greeks, slaves or free—and we were all made to drink of one Spirit. Indeed, the body does not consist of one member but of many.
>
> 1 CORINTHIANS 12: 12-14

The ancient prophets clearly predicted a remarkable effusion of the Holy Spirit that would accompany the Messianic period (Jl. 2:28). Before Christ's crucifixion , He promised to send a Comforter, who is the Holy Spirit, to instruct and guide His Church (Jn. 14.). After His resurrection, Jesus said to His disciples, "These signs shall follow them that believe. In my name shall they cast out devils; they shall speak with new tongues; they shall take up serpents; and if they drink any deadly thing, it shall not hurt them; they shall lay hands on the sick, and they shall recover" (Mk. 16:17, 18). Immediately before His ascension, Jesus said to the disciples, "Ye shall be baptized with the Holy Spirit not many days hence" (Acts 1:5). Accordingly, on the day of Pentecost, these promises and prophecies were literally fulfilled.[55]

The reality of what Jesus promised was nothing more than the infusion of the gifts of the Spirit. They were not confined to any one class of people, but extended to all classes—male and female, young and old; and secondly, in a wonderful diversity of supernatural endowments. Under circumstances so extraordinary, it was unavoidable that many disorders would arise. Some men would claim to be the organs of the Spirit, who were deluded or impostors; some would be dissatisfied with the gifts that they had received, and envy those whom they regarded as more highly favored; others would be inflated, and make an ostentatious display of their extraordinary powers; and in the public assemblies it might be expected that the greatest confusion would arise from so many persons being desirous to exercise their gifts at the same time. To the correction of these evils, all of which had manifested themselves in the church of Corinth, the Apostle Paul devoted three chapters.[56]

> *Without His aid we can do nothing: but by Him the weakest is made strong and is enabled to do all things that are required at his hands.*[66]

Unity, not Uniformity

The Holy Spirit had come, just as Jesus said it would. Extraordinary and diverse gifts were given to the followers of Christ; however, the people did not know how to effectively use them for God's glory. Chaos and confusion filled the church; what was supposed to be a gift for the Body quickly became a power grab for the gifted individual. The Body of Christ was in desperate need of unity in diversity.

Life is a balance between unity and diversity. Unity without diversity would produce uniformity, and uniformity tends to produce death. As a human

---

55   John Peter Lange et al., *A Commentary on the Holy Scriptures: 1 Corinthians* (Bellingham, WA: Logos Bible Software, 2008), 247.

56   Lange et al., *A Commentary on the Holy Scriptures*, 247.

body weakens, its systems slow down, and everything tends to become uniform. The ultimate end, of course, is that the body itself turns to dust. This helps to explain why some churches (and other Christian ministries) have weakened and died: there was not sufficient diversity to keep unity from becoming uniformity. Dr. Vance Havner says, "First there is a man, then a movement, then a machine, and then a monument."[57] Many ministries that began as a protest against dead orthodoxy have become dead themselves, because in their desire to remain pure and doctrinally sound they stifled creativity and new ideas.[58]

However, if diversity is not kept under control, it could destroy unity, and then you have anarchy. The tension in the body between individual members and the total organism can only be solved by maturity. Using the human body as his illustration, Paul explained three important facts about diversity in the Body of Christ:

1. The body needs different functions if it is to live, grow, and serve (vv. 14–20)

2. The members promote unity as they discover their dependence on one another (vv. 21–26)

3. Diversity of members fulfills the will of God in the body (vv. 27–31).[59]

Paul's opening words, *just as*, makes it clear that he is using the body as an analogy or metaphor for understanding the relationship between the diverse members of the Christian community. So it is with Christ; Christ is shorthand for the church as the Body of Christ (12:28). He leaves it to the reader to complete the thought: Just as the body has many limbs and organs, and despite their number and differences make up one body, so Christ's Body has many limbs and organs, and despite their number and differences make up one body.[60]

---

57   Warren W. Wiersbe, *The Bible Exposition Commentary*, vol. 1 (Wheaton, IL: Victor Books, 1996), 609–610.

58   Wiersbe, *The Bible Exposition Commentary*, 609–610.

59   Wiersbe, *The Bible Exposition Commentary*, 609–610.

60   Roy E. Ciampa and Brian S. Rosner, *The First Letter to the Corinthians*, The Pillar New Testament Commentary (Grand Rapids, MI: William B. Eerdmans Publishing Company, 2010), 589–598.

The word "part" is often translated as "member". The latter is a perfectly appropriate translation as long as it is kept in mind that "member" in this case would mean a part or organ of the human body, and not in the sense of a member of a social organization or church-member. Paul is not the first to use the body as a metaphor to explain the nature of a social group. In fact, it was a very common rhetorical device. However, Paul's use of it is significantly different from the way it was typically employed.[61]

It is also important to stress that the body metaphor or analogy is not used to impose uniformity upon the church. There is unity in plurality, but not uniformity. Individual integrity remains. Indeed, Paul's insistence that a functioning body needs diverse body parts reminds us of the need to distinguish and not equate solidarity and sameness.[62]

In Paul's mind there is some sense in which the divinely constructed union (v. 13) of the many diverse parts—organically interrelated; interdependently, harmoniously and functionally one body—constitutes now through the Holy Spirit the reality of Christ's visible presence and activity in the world. It is important to note that it is the historical, empirical church of Christ in the world, not some ideal, invisible, heavenly model, that is the real Body of Christ (vv. 12, 27).[63]

Being united to Christ in his incarnate reality, the Church constitutes the sanctified community within which we may draw near to the Father through the Son and in the Spirit and share in the eternal life, light, and love of God. That was surely the primary truth embedded in the mind and worship of the Catholic Church in the fourth century, and was rightly given precedence over all questions of external form, organization, and structure. It was, as they believed, the empirical Church that had been incorporated into Christ as his Body, the real structure of the Church as lodged in Christ himself, and had to be lived out in space and time through union and communion with the risen, exalted and advent Lord whose kingdom will have no end.[64]

---

61   Ciampa and Rosner, *The First Letter to the Corinthians*, 589–598.

62   Ciampa and Rosner, *The First Letter to the Corinthians*, 589–598.

63   Alan F. Johnson, *1 Corinthians*, vol. 7, The IVP New Testament Commentary Series (Downers Grove, IL: InterVarsity Press, 2004), 230–232.

64   Johnson, *1 Corinthians*, 230–232.

One Spirit, One Body

The body metaphor points to an ontological reality that Paul describes in the next verse: baptized by one Spirit so as to form one body (v. 13). Just what is this Spirit baptism? Early Pentecostal writers held that subsequent to salvation, the believer could experience the baptism of the Holy Spirit, and speak in tongues as evidence of it, in a similar manner as the original apostles on the day of Pentecost (Acts 2). More recent Pentecostal scholars see this verse as referring to our receiving the Spirit when we become Christians (Fee 1987:605), and speaking in tongues may be one evidence among others (e.g., the fruit of love, joy, peace) of this special baptism of the Spirit.[65]

Charles Simeon's perspective is that one soul pervades the whole body and operates alike in every part; calling into activity the eye, the ear, the hand, and the foot, and working by all according to their respective capacities. So, whether it be a king upon his throne, or a beggar on a dunghill, if he be truly alive to God, he is quickened by the same Spirit; the whole Church being, in its collective capacity, the Body of Christ, the fullness of Him that fills all in all. Without His aid we can do nothing: but by Him the weakest is made strong and is enabled to do all things that are required at his hands.[66]

Likewise, C. K. Barrett suggests that baptism signifies dying and rising with Christ; by this means the Christian, not in himself but in Christ, experiences the eschatological events of suffering and vindication which were anticipated in the events of Good Friday and Easter. In Christ he is a new creature, belonging to a new age, though this becomes factually apparent only partially, and through the sanctifying work of the Spirit. If, however, the Christian has in baptism put on Christ, so have other Christians too (Gal. 3:27); if the Spirit is now at work creating the image of Christ in and upon him, the same Spirit is at work in and for other Christians too. Hence there comes into being the Body, which belongs to Christ (v. 27), which is in Christ (Rom. 12:5), since all Christians who have put on Christ are one person in Him (Gal. 3:28). Not by nature, as the Stoics taught, nor by a mystic *gnosis*, but by

---

65   Johnson, *1 Corinthians*, 230–232.

66   Charles Simeon, *Horace Homileticae: 1 and 2 Corinthians*, vol. 16 (London, UK: Holdsworth and Ball, 1833), 308.

grace, men are incorporated into the cosmic unity. By nature, on the contrary, they are essentially diverse from and alien to one another: Jews and Greeks, slaves and free.[67]

According to Barrett, Paul's main intention is practical; the various national and social groups, and the dissident religious cliques at Corinth (1:11 f.), have all entered the unity of the body of Christ –which they ought to express, and not deny, by means of their various gifts. The exuberance of spiritual phenomena must not be suppressed—Paul never suggests this, though it might have been the easy way out of a problem—but harnessed to this end.[68]

The primary point is now established. Christians, who are members of Christ, constitute one Body, Christ's Body. This is one metaphorical way of describing the Church, but among Paul's metaphors (planting, building, and so forth) it holds an important place, and Paul proceeds to develop it. The first thing he notes about a body (in relation to the Corinthian situation) is its diversity. Christians should not expect to have identical gifts (this proposition is implied by the *for* with which the next clause begins); a body (not specifically Christ's body, but any body: generic use of the article in Greek) does not consist of (literally, *is not*) one member, but many. The point is made explicitly (cf. Plato, *Protagoras* 330A:). Each one has its proper function, like the parts of the face; an eye is not like the ears, nor is its function the same. God has put the members, each several one of them, in the body, as he saw fit. If the whole were one member (cf. verse 17), where would the body be? It would simply not exist as a body. But in fact, there are many members, and one body. This is true of the human body,

> *A critical component in developing the Beloved Community is teaching people in our congregations how to value one another as people of sacred worth, and how to value the gifts that each has been given.*

---

67   C. K. Barrett, *The First Epistle to the Corinthians*, Black's New Testament Commentary (London, UK: Continuum, 1968), 288–289.

68   Barrett, *The First Epistle to the Corinthians*, 288–289.

with which all Paul's readers are familiar; it is true also of the Christian Body: God wills its variety.[69]

To summarize the discussion on the Body of Christ, every baptized believer in Christ shares one Spirit and therefore has been incorporated into one new man who partakes of the resurrection life in which the former distinctions no longer carry the same significance. All those who have been united to Christ have become part of the same body—Christ's Body. When Paul develops his picture of the Church as the Body of the Messiah, he seems to be aware that this is not a metaphor chosen at random. Rather,

> What the creator God has accomplished in and through Jesus is the renewal of the human race, that for which humankind was made in the first place. What better image, then, to use for its corporate life than that of a human body, with limbs and organs working as they were meant to do? The present unity of the church is important not least because it will thereby anticipate the perfect harmony of the resurrection world, when members of the *soma Christou*, the Messiah's body, who have each exercised their *pneumatika*, spiritual gifts, are finally raised to life, to be given the *soma pneumatikon* (15:44–46), the entire body energized and animated by the divine Spirit.[70]

The Bible is the key and critical component to the development of the Beloved Community in today's world, even if it must begin in one neighborhood at a time. Dr. Martin Luther King, Jr. defined the Beloved Community in this way:

> The Beloved Community is a global vision in which all people can share in the wealth of the earth. In the Beloved Community, poverty, hunger, and homelessness will not be tolerated because international standards of human decency will not allow it. Racism and all forms of discrimination, bigotry, and prejudice will be replaced by an all-inclusive spirit of sisterhood and brotherhood.[71]

69   Barrett, *The First Epistle to the Corinthians*, 289–290.

70   Ciampa and Rosner, *The First Letter to the Corinthians*, 595.

71   "The Beloved Community: Martin Luther King Jr.'s Prescription for a Healthy Society," December 6, 2017, *Huff Post*, accessed September 22, 2018, https://www.huffingtonpost.com/jeffrey-ritterman/the-beloved-community-dr-_b_4583249.html.

Both of these Scripture passages clearly point us towards important truths in creating the Beloved Community. First, Leviticus teaches us that before we can consider building a Beloved Community, people must be willing to observe the commands and laws of God. People must be taught that Sabbatical seasons and the Year of Jubilee were established so that people would fully depend on God for provisions during seasons of rest. The biblical narrative reminds us of God's redemption, God's love, God's plan of salvation, and ultimately God's plan for His Kingdom to reign on earth as in heaven.

1 Corinthians 12 reminds us of the need to work together in unity and to celebrate the varied gifts and abilities that God has given to us individually to be used collectively as Christ's Body; the Church. Regardless of the number of resources we acquire in an attempt to build God's kingdom, we must always be aware of the importance of unity within diversity. We must always be mindful that we do not allow unity to become uniformity, for when this happens, we will surely die.

A critical component in developing the Beloved Community is teaching people in our congregations how to value one another as people of sacred worth, and how to value the gifts that each has been given. Providing opportunities to celebrate this diversity is God's desire for His Church. Just as in the church at Corinth, order had to be established so people could see the potential of using their gifts collectively; we too must seek to teach order and the benefits of collaborative and cooperative diversity in the Body of Christ.

Next, let's look at the historical foundations of the Beloved Community from the Reformation period until today.

Discipleship Is Not Disciple-Making

The definition of the Beloved Community is a community comprised of integrated worship, social services, youth programs, and civic engagement initiatives that operate within the church. New Jericho Christian Church is on mission to create a Beloved Community through collaborative and cooperative diversity while developing the Body of Christ.

But what have these ideas meant to the Church in previous times? For the Church to be transformed from a corporate mindset to becoming disciples of Christ who follow a biblical model for building the Kingdom, we also need to look at what we can learn from those in the past. As we explore these historical foundations, we will focus on the areas of disciple-making, mission, and outreach in the Church throughout history, as well as the Church's involvement in community organizations. Finally, we will look at the Beloved Community and how it has evolved and made progress up to and including the twenty-first century.

DISCIPLESHIP: A BRIEF HISTORY

The process of discipleship began when Jesus called twelve men and said, "Follow me, and I will make you fishers of men." From that very moment, the process of making disciples began to take shape. Three years later, Jesus completed the work that God entrusted to Him, which included miracles of healing, feeding, and raising the dead. Because Jesus' ministry was juxtaposed to the religious leaders of His day, He was set up and crucified on a cross for a crime He did not commit. From a prophetic perspective, it was foretold that Jesus would die for the sin of the world and be raised in three days. The prophecy was fulfilled, and now the narrative moved from death on a cross to the Mount of Olives, in preparation for Jesus' ascension to heaven. Prior to the ascension, Jesus gave his disciples instructions for building God's kingdom until His coming again in final victory. These instructions were called the Great Commission (Mt 28:16-20).

After giving the Great Commission to His disciples, we are told in the book of Acts that on the day of Pentecost, the Holy Spirit fell on those who gathered in an upper room. That day, the Church was born and the beginning of generative disciple-making also began. However, in order to understand discipleship in the context of the Great Commission, we must think about the historical background and current cultural paradigms that implicitly inform and under-gird our concepts of discipleship—and discover how they are hindering our fulfillment of the Great Commission today.[72]

First, we need to consider and study the history of how disciples were made within the context of the Christian Church. Directly linked to how disciples were made was how people of the Bible days thought about education. Because the church's level of creativity was similar to the culture around it, the way the culture thought about education became the way the church thought about it.

Many scholars have written extensively about how Paul made disciples. For the sake of brevity, the primary methods were:

1.   In a community or town, where all persons participated;

2.   By apprenticeship; this was the main method of education; and

3.   By increasing one's union with God in all aspects of life.

These foundational characteristics remained intact until about 300 AD, when Constantine entered the narrative and created the separation between clergy and laity. Suddenly and catastrophically, we abandoned the concept of discipling everybody equally and giving everyone equal standing as disciple-makers. It became the clergy's responsibility to be educated and trained, and everyone else's responsibility to follow them. It was a concept that was seldom challenged for over 1700 years.[73]

In 300 AD, people were trained to become clergy under strict guidelines. Although training for clergy positions was underway, it was taking place in

---

72   Jessie Cruickshank, "A Quick Educational History of Discipleship," accessed October 10, 2018, https://www.100movements.com/articles/a-quick-educational-history-on-discipleship.
73   Cruickshank, "A Quick Educational History of Discipleship."

an illiterate society. Therefore, people were not expected to learn from textbooks; rather, they learned the process of becoming disciples through stories and encounters in the spiritual realm. During that time, the world was enchanted, magical, mystical—full of angels, omens, relics, and supernatural encounters.[74]

Apprenticeship as a means of education remained, but it was an isolating experience. For example, if someone became interested in ministry, wanted to learn more about God, or had an interest in spiritual things, they would leave and attend a monastery. There, they would learn how to read and write; they would also be taken away and secluded from the rest of society in order to be trained. Moreover, their practice was not for everybody, and there were few people there to discuss ideas with. Essentially it evolved into an isolated process of education. Discipleship as Jesus spoke of did not exist; rather, individuals were trained in a mystical profession.[75]

If discipleship that leads to disciple-making is to be successful and reach its maximum effect, it must be communal, a process that can be executed by every person, in every place, and at every time.

During the Enlightenment Period in the 1500s and 1600s, the world made a significant change in education. People began to learn how to read and take a keen interest in the Bible. Yet the clergy-laity split continued, with the clergy wielding great power and influence over how people read the Bible. Many people who would read the Bible and come up with different conclusions were killed, and massacres of various religious groups became common. In fact, for the first 200 years of the Protestant Reformation up until 1900, the practice of killing and massacres continued. What was most discouraging was that in the face of human sacrifice in the name of religion, there still remained little to no value in making disciples of every person.[76]

---

74 Cruickshank, "A Quick Educational History of Discipleship."
75 Cruickshank, "A Quick Educational History of Discipleship."
76 Cruickshank, "A Quick Educational History of Discipleship."

As the varying Christian sects articulated their differing theologies, theology itself became an academic pursuit. In order to gain clergy status, one had to read, study, and become an academic, resulting in faith and discipleship losing their mystical quality. They lost their enchantment and became rational, Western, and Aristotelian. Instead of mystery, the Western world gained knowledge by measuring and defining. In the Enlightenment era, society believed nothing existed unless it could be measured, defined, and explained. People believed they could know the quality of what exists by how they measured it. This included God and faith; consequently society developed a new science called theology.[77]

The Western world began to build schools, seminaries, and universities where students studied theology, hermeneutics, and exegesis. In this era, the pursuit of God took the shape of looking at one's own understanding of scripture in order to discover the truth. Different people came up with ways to interpret the Bible, expanding theological understanding. The study of theology included learning Greek and Hebrew, but at its foundation, the pursuit of God was purely academic. In the Enlightenment, it was realized that man was smart and could study the things of the past and build on previous knowledge. People were able to interact with the world to measure and analyze it. Great men and women determined how the heavens were made, and the ways the stars and celestial bodies were laid out. They discovered and invented the sciences of physics, calculus, and many other mathematical means. The result was that the spiritual components were removed from clergy development and became an academic pursuit.[78]

The corresponding result in society was that disciple-making also in turn became an academic pursuit, and was taught by educating people in the books of the Bible, in what they knew of biblical times and culture, and learning biblical languages. However, discipleship for every person had little value beyond Christian education. Clergy status became less of a calling, and more of a vocation, like being a physicist. It lost its enchantment quality.[79]

---

77 Cruickshank, "A Quick Educational History of Discipleship."
78 Cruickshank, "A Quick Educational History of Discipleship."
79 Cruickshank, "A Quick Educational History of Discipleship."

Over the last thirty years, methods and processes for making disciples have gotten remarkably better; however, the principle of individual disciple-making has stayed the same. Somehow, we have not broken free from individualism and reengaged the principles of disciple-making that Jesus taught his disciples and desires of us.

Currently, most churches are using one of three basic processes of making disciples:

1. The mass-produced member—The discipleship process is really a membership process, focused around membership classes, information about the denomination of the church, and how to become a church member. This is an extremely common method.

2. The HR-recruitment strategy—This is where you may or may not have membership classes, but you need people to staff and volunteer the roles within a church. You need ushers, hospitality teams, and Sunday school teachers. The discipleship process invites people to connect, giving them a ministry gifts test, and then plugging them into the church ministry that seems like the best fit for them.[80]

3. The book or curriculum strategy— The curriculum is usually a book, which is often paired with a workbook with some great teaching videos. In this paradigm, reading books together and discussing them make disciples. This is a very teacher-esque philosophy of discipleship. However, it does not meet everybody's needs.[81]

If discipleship that leads to disciple-making is to be successful and reach its maximum effect, it must be communal, a process that can be executed by every person, in every place, and at every time. If your philosophy of discipleship or your method of discipleship focuses on everybody coming to church, then it is not a movement. If your philosophy or process of discipleship involves everybody going to a specific home group or hearing from a specific teacher, then it is not a movement.[82]

---

80   Cruickshank, "A Quick Educational History of Discipleship."
81   Cruickshank, "A Quick Educational History of Discipleship."
82   Cruickshank, "A Quick Educational History of Discipleship."

If our philosophy or process of discipleship cannot happen from any person to any other person, then we have missed it. We have missed the meaning of the Great Commission. If we require our disciple-makers to have a seminary degree or amazing theology in order to make disciples, then it is not a movement and we have thought too highly of our own theology. There cannot be a requirement to come to a specific place. There cannot be a level of maturity that is required in order to make disciples. If we do that, we have missed the beauty of Jesus promising to be truth incarnate in our midst. And we have missed the threshold of what it means to be a disciple-maker, which is not a call to a specific level of education or to a specific power of calling, but to everyone.[83]

Our discipleship process has to grow beyond our concepts of education in our society. It must be something that becomes much more viral, much more like a movement, much less rigid, much more enchanted, and much more dependent upon the Holy Spirit to lead us, guide us, and speak through us. Only the Holy Spirit can make a disciple of an immature believer—and it is supposed to be that way.

DISCIPLESHIP IS NOT DISCIPLE-MAKING

We have looked at the history of discipleship and discovered that in 300 AD, a significant shift in the Great Commission occurred during the time of Constantine that changed the purpose and process of making disciples in an unhealthy way. This shift was based on the move from communal discipleship to individualism. When we move in unity as an organism, we not only have traction: we multiply disciples rather than adding them. When we make disciples based on individualism, we develop models of addition where each individual can decide whether they choose to participate in the ministry of disciple-making. The multiplication model is grounded in a church or entire ministry seeing itself as capable of making disciples. The difference between the two is unprecedented.

According to scripture, after Pentecost there was a groundswell of people who accepted Christ as Savior and joined the first church. The Apostle Paul's ministry was successful in part because he established churches for the entire community.

83   Cruickshank, "A Quick Educational History of Discipleship."

His mission was to establish churches to meet the needs of all the people surrounding the church. During Paul's day, it was expected that everyone had a responsibility of making the gospel of Jesus Christ known; it was never Paul's intent to draw selected people to Christ, but rather "whosoever would, so let them come." Today, because of individualism, we have adopted a highly selective means and philosophy for becoming members of the church; everyone is not always welcomed. This has led to a sharp reduction in overall churchgoers, although there are a larger number of people who say they believe in Jesus Christ.

In 1850, a man by the name of Charles Adams was the first to separate evangelism from disciple-making. Evangelism, stemming from the Greek word euangelizomai, became synonymous with bringing people to Christ; and discipleship became synonymous with growing people in Christ. By separating these as two parts of the disciple-making mandate of the Great Commission, people began to prioritize one as more important than the other. Some prioritized evangelism, while others prioritized discipleship. However, both discipleship and evangelism are like two wings of an airplane. When people are flying at 30,000 feet in a commercial airliner and look out the window of the airplane, they do not argue that one wing is more important than the other. Both wings are critical. So it is with disciple-making.[84]

When Jesus commanded us to "Go and make disciples", He was not saying, "Go and do discipleship"; nor was He saying, "Go and do evangelism". He was saying *"Go and make disciples"* (emphasis mine), and that involved the whole process of winning people to Christ (evangelism), growing them in Christ (discipleship), and then sending them out to repeat the process.[85]

> *Mission was not made for the Church: the Church was made for mission— God's mission.[91]*

Dave Earley and Rod Dempsey have said, "The Great Commission has been worshiped, but not obeyed. The church has tried to get world evangelization

---

84   "The Distinction Between Discipleship and Disciple Making," *Facts & Trends,* September 11, 2014, accessed October 17, 2018, https://factsandtrends.net/2014/09/11/the-distinction-between-discipleship-disciple-making-a-qa-with-dann-spader/.

85   "The Distinction Between Discipleship and Disciple Making."

without disciple-making."[86] Disciple-making in its purest form is helping people find Jesus and then helping them to grow and become all they can be for Christ. In turn, they become committed to following His commands and obeying the Great Commission.[87]

The goal of disciple-makers is for God's name to be glorified. We accomplish this goal by getting people to operate by God's agenda. Moving people onto God's agenda involves helping them discover and experience God's will for their lives.[88] Discipleship is a part of the disciple-making journey, but just one part. Biblical disciple-making involves the whole process of winning the lost, building the believer, equipping the worker, and sending out proven multipliers. This was the original intent of Jesus when He gave the Great Commission. This is what Jesus so masterfully modeled for us.[89]

In order for the church to be realigned to God's plan to build God's kingdom, it has to purge misguided learned behaviors and reestablish the true meaning of the Great Commission. This is not a one-time effort; rather it becomes a new way of being, and a new way of life for the whole congregation. Without making this necessary shift, the church will continue along a path of individualism, where members get to choose if they are going to participate with God or not. Ultimately, if the church does not participate in God's plan to build His kingdom, the church will stall, plateau, and ultimately die.

MISSION WAS NOT MADE FOR THE CHURCH

Disciple-making is the desire of God as commanded by Jesus in the Great Commission. As disciples are made, they must find viable places within the life of the church to serve as a means of glorifying God; this is the definition of mission.

When we talk about mission, we must first understand the biblical meaning of mission rather than what we have allowed mission to become. "Fundamentally,

---

86   Dave Earley, Rod Dempsey, *Disciple Making Is . . .: How to Live the Great Commission with Passion and Confidence* (Nashville, TN: B&H Publishing Group, 2013), 1.

87   Earley, Dempsey, *"Disciple Making Is."* Loc. 343-345.

88   Earley, Dempsey, *"Disciple Making Is."* Loc. 354-356.

89   "The Distinction Between Discipleship and Disciple Making."

our mission (if it is biblically informed and validated) means our committed participation as God's people, at God's invitation and command, in God's own mission within the history of God's world for the redemption of God's creation."[90] God's mission is to redeem God's people for the New Creation. It is not so much that God has a mission for the Church in the world, as that God has a church for His mission in the world. Mission was not made for the Church: the Church was made for mission—God's mission.[91]

There should be no theology that does not relate to the mission of the Church— either by being generated out of the Church's mission or by inspiring and shaping it. Likewise, there should be no mission of the Church carried on without deep theological roots in the soil of the Bible. There should be no theology without missional impact, and no mission without theological foundations.[92]

Throughout the first two eras of the modern missionary movement, beginning with William Carey in the eighteenth century and ending sometime in the latter half of the last century, the definition of missions was clear: missions was the job of missionaries who traveled overseas, who had a lifetime commitment to bring the gospel message to those who had never heard. The role of mission committees in the churches was to support the missionaries in their task, and the distinction between missions and other ministries in the church was clear. However, times have changed. Short-term mission teams abound, the world and its variety of religions have come to our doorstep, and the West has been recognized as a legitimate mission field. Amid such change and diversity, churches have become somewhat unclear in distinguishing missions from the other ministries in the church. Indeed, at times, the distinction has been deliberately downplayed in order to encourage every believer to be a missionary wherever they are.[93]

---

90   Christopher J. H. Wright, *The Mission of God: Unlocking the Bible's Grand Narrative,* (Downers Grove: IL Intervarsity Press, 2006), 23.

91   _____. *The Mission of God's People: A Biblical Theology of the Church's Mission* (Grand Rapids, MI: Zondervan Publishing, 2010), 24.

92   Wright, *The Mission of God's People,* 26.

93   Mark Naylor, "The Difference between Missions and Outreach," *Cross Cultural Impact for the 21st Century,* December 1, 2008, accessed October 17, 2018, http://impact.nbseminary.com/the-difference-between-missions-and-outreach/.

To further clarify the purpose and call to mission, consider the following scripture text from Acts 13:2-4:

> While they were worshiping the Lord and fasting, the Holy Spirit said, "Set apart for me Barnabas and Saul for the work to which I have called them." So after they had fasted and prayed, they placed their hands on them and sent them off. The two of them, sent on their way by the Holy Spirit, went down to Seleucia and sailed from there to Cyprus.

The distinction between other ministries of the church and missions is clear in this passage. The church at Antioch had a responsibility to be Christ's witness in their local context, but they were also given the opportunity to affirm with the Holy Spirit that some are *set apart for a distinct task that is fulfilled beyond the boundaries of the church.* That is, Paul and Barnabas were sent out to initiate the kingdom in a context where the Church had no influence. The Church did not directly benefit or grow numerically through this process. On the contrary, they sacrificed their best and brightest in order to see God's work become established and grow among a group separate from themselves. This understanding of missions does not necessarily require geographical distance, but it does require the appointing of individuals to the task of stepping beyond the boundaries of the local church's influence in order to *initiate the Kingdom where it would not otherwise occur.*[94] The remaining members are charged by the Great Commission to make disciples in the community where they are planted. All members are required by the Lord to make disciples. This is not up for negotiation; it was the last command of Jesus.

Churches must grow to make a distinction between their task of local outreach and evangelism and their role in missions. Consider the following statements:

A church is little more than a mirror of the surrounding culture where relationships are disposable and selfish consumerism is god.[100]

---

94   Naylor, "The Difference between Missions and Outreach."

- *Outreach* is making an impact where you live; *missions* is making an impact by intentionally stepping beyond where you live.

- *Evangelism* is the church growing where it is; missions is the church going where it is not.

- *Outreach* is what the church does by existing within its context; *missions* is what the church does by initiating beyond its context.[95]

There is no doubt that the Bible demonstrates the sending of many people on a mission from God, and the missionary movement in the book of Acts begins with a church responding to that divine impulse by sending Paul and Barnabas out on their first missionary journey. Mission arises from the heart of God and is communicated from God's heart to ours. Mission is the global outreach of a global people of a global God.[96]

A FAMILY OR A SHOPPING MALL?

When it comes to the modern Church, it seems that more Evangelicals are concerned about the decline of marriage as a covenant commitment than we are about the decline of the Church as a covenant community. We take a strong moral stand against living together and breaking our marriage vows. Yet in our covenant relationships in the Body of Christ, we are more permissive, making and breaking promises with hardly a blush.[97]

Before a church can forge meaningful relationships with the community where it is planted, it must first heal the wounds, scars, and pain that exist among its members within the church. Especially in the urban core, an unhealthy church is in no position to minister and meet the relevant needs of the people outside its doors.

---

95   Naylor, "The Difference between Missions and Outreach."

96   Wright, *The Mission of God's People*, 42.

97   David Dyck, "Why Not Just Live Together?: Some Reflections on Covenant Community" *Direction 30*, no. 2 (Fall 2001): 211–16, accessed October 18, 2018, http://proxy.payne.edu:2061/login. aspx?direct =true&db=rfh&AN=ATLA 000138 0042 &site=ehost-live.

This is a condition that has become all too common in churches and communities throughout the United States of America.

Many experts initially posited that when neighborhood members moved away to more affluent communities because of upward mobility, they also distanced themselves from what were once their neighbors. Although upward mobility has allowed many to escape the challenges of the urban core, this is not always the case: members can continue to maintain their relationship with their church by driving in for programs, activities, and worship, while disregarding the people who lived just outside the doors of the church.

This behavior reinforces individualism in the sense that upward mobility causes those who are able to move out to disregard those who remain in the community. Even though they were blessed to move to better neighborhoods, they still have a responsibility to disciple and meet the needs of those who are less fortunate.

The Church once prided itself on being the best example of community; today it has changed its perspective, and as a result, a visible decline in congregational relationships is evident. The main reason for this decline is that our vision of the Church has quietly changed. At one time, the best metaphor to describe the Church was a family. In the past, the Church was a body of believers who were bound together with the kind of commitments and loyalties that one finds in a family. Relationships were deeply rooted as members worked, worshiped, and resolved conflict together. It was by no means perfect, but even in that regard it resembled a family.[98]

Today the concept of church as family has changed. While many churches still call themselves a family, they more closely resemble a shopping mall. The Church has become an outlet for religious consumers wanting religious services that meet their felt needs. The degree to which their felt needs are met determines their level of commitment. If a more exciting offer comes along, or if relationships become a little strained, there is always another outlet in close proximity to provide them with the same or similar services.

Sociologist Robert Wuthnow describes it this way:

> The kind of community in the church today is quite different from the communities in which people lived in the past. These

---

98   Dyck, "Why Not Just Live Together?."

communities today are more fluid, and the social contract bind-
ing members together asserts only the weakest of obligations. It
reflects the fluidity of our lives by allowing us to bond simply, but
to break our attachments with equivalent ease.[99]

When members find it easy to separate themselves from the Church based
on systemic issues that confront them, God's vision for covenant relationships is the
answer. Just as God intended couples to live in covenant relationships through marriage rather than just living together, He intended the same for church members.
God had something far better in mind than the "easy-come-easy-go" relationships
of a shopping mall. His intention was to form a redeemed community, a whole new
society, where His design for a New Creation was on display. Therefore, it is no small
thing when a church moves from being a family to becoming a mall outlet, and when
relationships in the Body of Christ become promiscuous. The gospel itself is at risk.
And a church is little more than a mirror of the surrounding culture where relationships are disposable and selfish consumerism is god.[100]

Dyck recommends four ways the Church can rebuild its internal relationships and return to living as a family—as God intended.

1. First, we need to confront some of the weaknesses of church growth
   theory. An unbridled strategy of growth is destroying covenant communities. Not all church growth is a blessing, or the sign of a healthy
   church. It may in fact be the sign of a flirtatious church that is willingly
   complicit in the promiscuous living of weak believers. We would not
   tolerate that behavior between married couples. Why then do we bless
   it in the covenant community?

2. To rebuild a covenant community, church leaders will need to immerse
   themselves in a biblical vision of the Church. One of the reasons the
   Church has become a mall outlet today is because marketing experts
   have taken over the imagination of many pastors. We have become far
   more literate in the world of niche marketing and strategic planning
   than we are in the gospels and the epistles. The result is a church that is
   reshaped in a consumer mold.

---

99   Dyck, "Why Not Just Live Together?."
100 Dyck, "Why Not Just Live Together?"

3. Our baptism and church membership ceremonies need to reflect both the personal and corporate dimension of disciple-making. Currently, many of these ceremonies focus mainly on the individual and his or her personal conversion story, and that is important. But there is an opportunity in this service to also emphasize the corporate dimension of the gospel and especially the meaning of covenant relationships.

4. We need to model the depth of relationship that Christ called us to in the New Creation. As noted above, the church as a covenant community is part of God's good news for a broken world. In our day, when promiscuity is rampant and relationships are disposable, the church can model a very different way of life.[101]

Once the internal relationships and covenant community is reestablished, the church can begin to extend itself to those who live in the community around it. An impactful way that the church can begin to meet the relevant needs of the community is by collaborating with community organizations. Although churches have always been the heart of community life, they have not always worked closely with other denominational or faith bodies, let alone with other institutions in the community. While admitting this varies widely from community to community and church to church, most would agree that there is an upswing in church involvement through community organizations.

Kimberly Bobo suggests six reasons why working with community organizations is a good idea for local churches:

1. Churches cannot solve the society-wide problems faced by their congregants without help. Churches do an excellent job of helping families deal with individual problems—one or two people without jobs, one person in prison, two people with drug or alcohol addictions, and one child who cannot read. Churches recruit volunteers to help people find jobs, visit someone in prison, counsel addicts, or tutor a child.

2. Churches join community organizations to learn how to develop strategies appropriate for addressing community-wide problems. Not only do churches recognize that the problems are too big for them to handle,

---

101   Dyck, "Why Not Just Live Together?"

but they require strategies and approaches with which churches are unfamiliar.

3. Congregations join community organizations to help rebuild their congregations. Many congregations get involved in community organizations because they view it as a way to help revitalize the congregation. Active involvement in community organizations provides visibility for the congregation, its pastors, and its leadership. Community organizations provide leadership-training opportunities that benefit people in the community and help church leaders be stronger leaders in the church.

4. Community organizations, even those that had not originally worked much with churches, are recognizing the potential power in congregations. Community groups are seeking out congregations in a way that they have not done in the past, in order to increase their numbers, credibility, and power by enlisting the support and involvement of neighborhood churches.

5. Some community organizations are encouraged by foundations to look more to churches as sources of power. Community organizations that are greatly dependent upon foundation dollars for support are highly attuned to the latest whim of the foundation dollars. If the dollars suggest churches as a key constituency, organizations respond.

6. Many denominations have discovered the rejuvenating power of community organizing and thus are strongly encouraging congregations to get involved in community organizing efforts. Denominations help encourage this congregation/community organizing partnership by funding church-based community organizing groups (sometimes to the tune of hundreds of thousands of dollars), funding clergy to attend organizing training schools, and promoting participation in community organizing efforts through denominational publications and conferences.[102]

---

102   Kimberley A. Bobo, 1995, "Church Involvement in Community Organizations," *Review & Expositor* 92 (1): 31–38, accessed October 18, 2018, http://proxy.payne.edu:2061/login.aspx ?direct= true&db=rfh&AN=ATLA0000893668&site=ehost-live.

Churches are becoming increasingly involved in community organizations—not just because it is a good thing to do, but because the congregations need the power, resources, experience, and direction they can gain from participating in a community organization. Like every joint endeavor, community organizations have their struggles, and each congregation that participates may have hurdles to overcome, but the outcome can be significant for the congregation and its members. We serve a God who cares about the whole human being and the whole community. As people of faith, we are called to care for the whole human being and the whole community. If we can best serve the congregation's members and the community at large by joining a community organization, so be it. In fact, this has been the case. Congregations are participating in larger numbers than ever before.[103]

ENTER THE BELOVED COMMUNITY

Martin Luther King, Jr. said, "Injustice anywhere is a threat to justice everywhere." The dominant Americans who trace their lineage to Europe have not yet fully comprehended the fact that the United States is a pluralistic society in every sense of the term. From the earliest times, the tacit assumption that Euro-Americans were destined and divinely ordained to dominate society, and that their culture was the most advanced (and therefore superior), has so conditioned the consciousness of this nation as to obscure its reality. There has always been a Black counterpoint to conventional expositions of the American religious experience. For the Church, this counterpoint is the Beloved Community: a community which (to paraphrase Martin Luther King, Jr.) accepts a person on the basis of the content of his or her character rather than upon the color of his or her skin.[104]

The Evangelical Church and the Beloved Community

The evangelicalism of the first third of the 19th century, which is frequently cited as a contributor to an emergent sense of national unity, did not function for

---

103   Bobo, "Church Involvement in Community Organizations."

104   Lawrence N. Jones, 1981. "Black Christians in Antebellum America: In Quest of the Beloved Community," *The Journal of Religious Thought* 38 (1): 12–19, accessed October 19, 2018, http:// proxy .payne.edu:2061/login.aspx?direct=true&db=rfh&AN=ATLA0000786280&site= ehost-live.

Blacks because they did not have the experience of being truly a part of the nation. The modest number of Blacks who were members of churches found in evangelicalism, and especially in the Bible, a basis for hope and a promise of eternal blessedness. They did not warrant full membership in the national community. Their suffering and their oppression because of race were their bond of unity. On the face of it, it was impossible for Evangelical Christianity to provide a source of unity in any but a cosmetic sense when they were excluded from the fellowship of the churches, physically segregated in church buildings, excluded for a long period from access to full ordination, restricted to ministering to their own people, organized into separate congregations, and permitted only token representation in national church bodies.[105]

The schizophrenia of churches and churchmen with respect to race, though there were notable exceptions, is one of the paradoxes of the religious history of America even to this day. Thus, for Blacks, the schisms of the churches were white folk's business, which did not effectually alter their lives. To be sure, Northern Blacks applauded the schisms as evidence of the movement of God in history, but they were under no illusion that it represented a change in the stance of the churches on Black's place in the scheme of things.[106]

All Men Are Created Equal

American society sees its strength as coming from its commitments to the Declaration of Independence and the Judeo-Christian tradition, meaning these sources have functioned as primary authorities in social and political arrangements. Yet they have been less potent in changing racist attitudes and the actions which flow from these attitudes. The early stigma that was attached to Blacks in America was that they, if human, were at the least an inferior species, and at best forever doomed to be aliens in this land. Thus the first priority of Blacks was to achieve acceptance as mature members of the human race. Thomas Jefferson articulated the position of most whites when he wrote:

---

105   Jones, "Black Christians in Antebellum America."
106   Jones, "Black Christians in Antebellum America."

I advance it, therefore, as a suspicion only, that the Blacks, whether originally a distinct race, or made distinct by time and circumstances, are inferior to whites in the endowment both of body and mind.[107]

Jefferson was too much of a scientist to make such a statement categorically, but it doubtless provided the basis for his relationship with Blacks. It is ironic that though Jefferson subscribed to theories of Black inferiority, he wrote into the Declaration the statement that became a watchword in the drive of Blacks for equality: "We hold these truths to be self-evident, that all men are created equal, and that they are endowed by the Creator with certain unalienable rights and that among these are life, liberty, and the pursuit of happiness."[108]

Blacks did not distinguish between sacred and secular in their quest for community. The issues of freedom and slavery, dignity as human beings, and sonship to God were too intertwined to admit to this kind of division. As a consequence of this holistic view of life, every activity that enhanced any aspect of their life was evaluated in terms of its contribution to moving the race toward full membership in the Beloved Community. Black Americans have always had a high concept of the church as an inclusive community—a primary expression of the Beloved Community. Evangelical Protestantism contributed to this concept by stressing the universality of the salvation wrought on Calvary. It provided one of the first clues to alien Blacks that in the eyes of God, at least, master-and-slave and Black-and-white distinctions were of no import.[109]

Though the impression may be created that their exclusion from the proximate Beloved Community condemned them to become otherworldly, this was not precisely the case. While Black religion had heaven in its view, it lived in expectation that the Kingdom would come on earth. Therefore, the coming of the Civil War was not due to the activity of human agents but to the initiative of God. It was an understanding of history as holy that provided the hermeneutic for the exegesis of

---

107   Jones, "Black Christians in Antebellum America."
108   Jones, "Black Christians in Antebellum America."
109   Jones, "Black Christians in Antebellum America."

the events of every day for Black Christians. They believed that God's justice and righteousness would ultimately triumph.[110]

Black Christians grounded their confidence in a theology of history. Their efforts were to actualize on earth the vision of the Beloved Community embodied in the Declaration of Independence and explicit in the Bible. They longed to see the Kingdom made concrete in history. The predominantly white churches lost sight of this goal even as the nation lost sight of the ideals enshrined in the Declaration of Independence. In response, the Black presence and struggle have been a constant judgment upon this loss of vision.[111]

A Transfiguring Love

Historians have underestimated both the philosophical novelty and the social impact of philosopher Josiah Royce's formulation of the Beloved Community, which he construed as the principle of all principles. While it may be true that his philosophy of loyalty sometimes shimmers with liberal hopes of human progress and perfectibility, as Charles Marsh puts it, "It would be a mistake to reduce Royce to the view that most of what one needs to know of God is discovered in ethical religion, slightly adjusted for churchgoers in capitalist economies."[112] For Royce, the Beloved Community "does not consist simply in making a transition from an individual to a social level, but in the establishment of that special community which does not breed individualism because it embodies something higher, and therefore, super-human form of love, powerful enough to transform the individual and at the same time, do away with the fatal outcome of natural social cultivation which is based on nothing higher than human talents and potentials."[113]

> *"Community cannot for long feed on itself. It can only flourish with the coming of others from beyond, their unknown and undiscovered brothers and sisters."[115]*

110   Jones, "Black Christians in Antebellum America."
111   Jones, "Black Christians in Antebellum America."
112   Jones, "Black Christians in Antebellum America."
113   Jones, "Black Christians in Antebellum America."

Royce understood in his own way that participating in a community united by love transforms the individual. This transfiguring relationship, this mystery of loving membership in a community whose meaning seems divine, is for Royce the specific condition of that particular authenticity that constitutes the graced or Beloved Community. Royce thought that religious communities allow us to carry on, even after serious defeat and loss, and to believe that our experience of finitude will not be the last word.[114]

Evil is Not Ultimate

The author and philosopher Howard Thurman sought to build a Beloved Community as a living confirmation or empirical validation of what he considered to be a profound religious and ethical insight concerning the genius of the church as a religious fellowship. While Thurman's vision of the Beloved Community was born out of his struggle against the exclusionary barriers that segregated, *de facto* if not *de jure*, white from Black Christian churches, an experience in San Francisco in 1944 broadened his vision by a glimpse into a radically non-exclusionary spiritual community. In 1944, he co-founded, along with Alfred Fisk, the first major interracial, interdenominational church in the United States. Of that experience Thurman said, "Community cannot for long feed on itself. It can only flourish with the coming of others from beyond, their unknown and undiscovered brothers and sisters."[115]

In ways analogous to Royce, Thurman believed that individuation consisted of expressions of sincere loyalty to some communal cause. "Commitment means that it is possible for a [person] to yield the nerve center of [his or her] consent to a purpose or a cause, a movement or an ideal, which may be more important to him [or her] than whether he [or she] lives or dies." Thurman insists: "If love is not operative, then community is impossible." To Thurman, those who are loyal to the Beloved Community are required to take evil seriously, but also to believe that it does not have the last word: "It is not ultimate. Even as evil is active in the lives of men and women, it becomes an ingredient for personal growth. It tests the moral fiber

---

114   Jones, "Black Christians in Antebellum America."
115   Jones, "Black Christians in Antebellum America."

of the person, and by stretching and straining makes the fiber stronger."[116]

The Beloved Community, for Thurman and all who were in the throes of the Civil Rights revolution, served as both a here-and-now experience of freedom—always within a social climate, the residue of which one retains even in solitude—and a radical moral imperative that steadfastly refused to separate the means open to revolution from the ends to be achieved by it. Thurman believed that "[t]he presence of the Beloved Community is always manifesting itself in the lives of people in the very midst of the social decay which surrounds them."[117]

> *The ground is pregnant with possibility for the Beloved Community to emerge as God intended.*

The End is Redemption

For Martin Luther King, Jr., writes Fluker, "All human life is interrelated and must be seen as a single process culminating in the Beloved Community." In his December 1956 address to the Montgomery Improvement Association at the Holt Street Baptist Church in Montgomery, King claimed that the boycott and its achievements did not in themselves represent the goal of the struggle: "The end is reconciliation, the end is redemption," King said, "the end is the creation of the Beloved Community."[118]

As we will explore in the next chapter, King's vision of the Beloved Community was grounded in a specific theological tradition, and no amount of postmodern complexity can remove that intention or claim. King's philosophical and theological interpretation as well as his pragmatic, if not also prophetic, application of the socio-ethical ideal of 'the Beloved Community' led him to proclaim in 1956 that the Montgomery Bus Boycott and its achievements did not, in themselves, represent the ultimate goal or final aim of the Civil Rights Movement. Similar to Thurman, King actively but nonviolently resisted—under conditions contaminated by

---

116   Jones, "Black Christians in Antebellum America."
117   Jones, "Black Christians in Antebellum America."
118   Jones, "Black Christians in Antebellum America."

violence and looming threats of racial violence, resulting not only in fear but also hatred and deception, all of which distort the personality—the injustices inherent in materialism, militarism, and racism.[119]

The Beloved Community envisioned by many is the hallmark of God's plan of redemption in the twenty-first century. God's mission on earth was to redeem His people from the vestiges of sin. Beginning with the promise God made to Abraham to make him the father of many nations, God has been working to redeem His people. As God led His people to the Land of Promise, He was also forming them to glorify Him as a way of life. The covenant that God made with Moses and the Israelites (known as the Ten Commandments) was a significant step toward eternal redemption. Leading the Israelites to a land unfamiliar to them, a land they did not own and that was occupied by others, served as the training and maturing ground for the Israelites to lean and depend on God for all they needed in life. This Land of Promise was emblematic of the Beloved Community; the land would provide everything the Israelites would need to live together in love and harmony with one another.

Jesus implemented the second phase of God's plan of redemption by dying for the sins of the world. In the death, burial, and resurrection of Jesus, the promise of everlasting life with God emerged. Although the struggle continued to establish God's Kingdom on earth, He was unceasingly faithful in moving His people forward. From a single people called the Israelites, God provided opportunities for Jews and Gentiles, slaves and free people, to be His people—the New Jerusalem, the New Creation, and the Beloved Community.

In the fullness of time, two significant obstacles arose in the land: slavery and racism. Again, God strengthened the resolve of oppressed people to withstand the actions of a majority culture resolved to keep God's people in bondage, similar to the days of the Pharaohs in Egypt. Even then, God made provisions for the emancipation of oppressed people; and today, the promised light of equality and freedom for all of God's people continues to shine.

The Great Commission of Jesus compels those who love and trust the Lord to make disciples of all nations. In this way, the United States has become a

---

119   Jones, "Black Christians in Antebellum America."

multicultural country with people of all races and hues living, serving, and worshiping like never before. What was once a dominant culture that lorded over others is slowly fading into the tapestry of a united nation under God. While there is more work to be done, and more people to receive the love of God that is found in Christ Jesus, the ground is pregnant with possibility for the Beloved Community to emerge as God intended. This will happen, because it is the will of God concerning God's people.

CHAPTER SEVEN

Divine Ownership and Divine Gift

In order to get a full picture of what we can learn from these sources, we will now take a moment to look more deeply at the theological foundations as they pertain to establishing the Beloved Community. We will now look at the theological foundations of Jubilee, the Beloved Community, and liberation theology.

The Ultimate Land-Lord

"The land shall not be sold permanently, for the land belongs to me; for you are 'guests' and 'residents' with me" (Lev. 25:23). This statement, at the heart of the chapter containing the Jubilee, provides the hinge between the social and economic system described above and its theological rationale. It makes two fundamental statements about the land Israel lived on, and about the Israelites themselves. These statements are crucial to understanding the rationale for the Jubilee.[120]

One of the central pillars of the faith of Israel was that the land they inhabited was YHWH's land. It had been His even before Israel entered it (Ex. 15:13,17). This theme of the divine ownership of the land is found often in the prophets and Psalms. Far more often than it is ever called 'Israel's land', it is referred to as 'YHWH's land.' At the same time, although it belonged to YHWH, the land had been promised and then given to Israel in the course of the redemptive history. It was their possession and their inheritance, as Deuteronomy repeatedly describes. Consequently, the land was in Israel's possession, but still under God's ownership. This dual tradition of the land (divine ownership and divine gift) was associated in some way with every major thread in Israel's theology.[121]

The promise of land was an essential part of the patriarchal election tradition. The land was the goal of the Exodus redemption tradition. The maintenance

---

120   Christopher J H. Wright, 2017, "Theology of Jubilee: Biblical, Social and Ethical Perspectives," *Evangelical Review of Theology* 41 (1): 6–18, accessed December 18, 2018, http://search.ebscohost.com.wilberforcepayne. idm.oclc.org/login.aspx?direct=true&db=rfh&AN =ATLAn4105437&site=ehost-live.
121   Wright, "Theology of Jubilee."

of the covenant relationship and the security of life in the land were bound together. Divine judgment eventually meant expulsion from the land, until the restored relationship was symbolized in the return to the land. The land, then, stood like a fulcrum in the relationship between God and Israel (notice, for example, its pivotal position in Lev. 26:40-45). The land was a monumental, tangible witness both to YHWH's control of history within which the relationship had been established, and to the moral demands on Israel which that relationship entailed. For the Israelite, living with his family on his allotted share of YHWH's land, the land itself was the proof of his membership of God's people and the focus of his practical response to God's grace. Nothing that concerned the land was free from theological and ethical dimensions—as every harvest reminded him (Dt. 26).[122]

"You are guests and residents (RSV), aliens and tenants (NIV) with me" (vs. 23). These terms, *gerim w'tosabim*, normally in Old Testament texts describe a class of people who resided among the Israelites in Canaan, but were not ethnic Israelites. They may have been descendants of the dispossessed Canaanites or immigrants. They had no stake in the tenure of the land, but survived by hiring out their services as residential employees (laborers, craftsmen, etc.) for Israelite land-owning households. Provided an Israelite household itself remained economically viable, then its resident alien employees enjoyed both protection and security. Otherwise, their position could be perilous. Hence these resident aliens are frequently mentioned in Israel's law as the objects of particular concern for justice because of their vulnerability.[123]

> *If Christ is King, he is king of everything. Both Jubilee and atonement are essentially about restoration, reuniting things that have been torn apart.*

The point of Leviticus 25:23 is that the Israelites were to regard their own status before God as analogous to that of these residential dependents to themselves. Just as they had resident guests living with them in the land that they (the Israelites)

---

122   Wright, "Theology of Jubilee."
123   Wright, "Theology of Jubilee."

owned, so they (the Israelites) were resident guests living on the land that YHWH owned. Thus, they (the Israelites) had no ultimate title to the land—it was owned by God. YHWH was the supreme landlord. Israel was His collective tenant. Nevertheless, the Israelites could enjoy secure benefits of the land under YHWH's protection and through dependence on Him. The terms are not (as they might sound in English) a denial of rights, but rather an affirmation of a relationship of protected dependency.[124]

The Jubilee was based upon several central affirmations of Israel's faith, and their importance should not be overlooked when assessing its relevance to Christian ethics and mission. As we observed with the Exodus, it would be quite wrong to limit the challenge of the Jubilee to the socioeconomic realm and ignore its inner spiritual and theological motivation. From a holistic missiological point of view, each is as important as the other, for all are fully biblical and all fully reflect the character and will of God. The fundamental theology behind it also lies behind our practice of evangelism: in fact, the assumptions are the same.[125]

The theological underpinning of the socio-economic legislation of the Jubilee is identical to that which undergirds the proclamation of the Kingdom of God. The Jubilee itself became a picture of the new age of salvation that the New Testament announces. It is an institution that models in a small corner of ancient Israelite economics the essential contours of God's wider mission for the restoration of humanity and creation. When appropriately set in the light of the rest of the biblical witness, the wholeness of the Jubilee model embraces the Church's evangelistic mission, its personal and social ethics, and its future hope.[126]

Jubilee Was for Everyone

Israel's Jubilee and Jubilee legislation did not just apply to the Israelites. They were also applicable to the long-term residents of the land. As previously noted, these resident aliens were objects of concern for justice because of their vulnerability - their well-being depended on the households they were associated with

---

124   Wright, "Theology of Jubilee."
125   Wright, "Theology of Jubilee."
126   Wright, "Theology of Jubilee."

as employees and slaves. The fact that the Israelites were commanded to care for their fellow Israelites who had fallen into poverty as they would a foreigner and a stranger (Lev. 25:35), and the way that this looked in practice, clearly implies that they were to treat the resident foreigners with compassion, justice and generosity. Indeed, as Wright points out, the Jubilee legislation describes the Israelites as aliens in God's land: their relationship to God is analogous to their resident aliens' relationship to them. Israel must, therefore, treat anyone who is impoverished in the way that God treats Israel. Other passages and commands support this, for example:

> Do not deprive the foreigner or the fatherless of justice or take the cloak of the widow as a pledge. Remember that you were slaves in Egypt of justice and the Lord your God redeemed you from there. That is why I command you to do this (Dt. 24:17-18).[127]

The whole of the Jubilee (liberation from slavery, restoration to home, family, and land) might have been primarily for the Israelite people, but this was to be extended to the non-Israelite members of the community and marked Israel as distinctive and different. It is unclear whether or not Israel ever fulfilled its Jubilee laws completely: certainly, by the time of the monarchy, Jubilee was not being upheld. What we see in the Old Testament is a narrative of Israel's inability to fully obey the law and assure their redemption and restoration on their own. The prophets explain Israel's fall as a consequence of their failures: Jeremiah 34 explicitly references how, in a Jubilee year, the Hebrew aristocracy freed their slaves but then promptly re-enslaved them. Jeremiah directly connects the fall of Jerusalem and the exile in Babylon to Israel's failure to uphold the Jubilee and seek justice. Other prophets of the Old Testament, most notably Isaiah, point to the One who would be able to fulfill the law and God's desire for redemption and restoration of His creation.[128]

Jubilee is Fulfilled in the Cross

As we continue to the New Testament, we must reflect on the impact of Christ's life, death, and resurrection on our understanding of Jubilee. This is essential

---

127 "Theology of Jubilee," *Tear Fund*, accessed December 18, 2018, https://www.tearfund. org/~ /media/files/wewontstop/theologyofjubilee, 2.
128 "Theology of Jubilee," *Tear Fund,* 3.

to thinking about its place in our lives as disciples today. One of the most commonly referenced passages in discussing Jesus' mission and His role in the mission of God comes from Luke 4: 16-20. Here Jesus is reading from Isaiah 61, which in turn refers to Leviticus 25 and the Jubilee laws. At this moment, Jesus announces that His mission is God's mission: the redemption of God's creation and the restoration of its relationship with God. This mission had begun with the covenant with Abraham, continued through the Exodus and the nation of Israel, and would be fulfilled by the Messiah as foretold by Isaiah. Jesus identifies Himself as this very Messiah and the fulfillment of Jubilee. In this He declares that his mission is proclaimed and enacted, spiritually and physically, for Israel and the nations.[129]

> *If Christ is King, he is king of everything. Both Jubilee and atonement are essentially about restoration, reuniting things that have been torn apart.*

In the New Testament, Jubilee and atonement are essentially linked in Jesus' life, death and resurrection. Here they are dramatically fulfilled in an even greater redemption than the one provided by the Jubilee laws. Through this, we learn that God's mission has even wider redemptive dimensions, and the gospel is good news for all of creation. The cross is important across the whole of missions, because the whole of missions confronts the powers of evil and the kingdom of Satan. If Christ is King, He is king of everything. Both Jubilee and atonement are essentially about restoration, reuniting things that have been torn apart. Moreover, the fulfillment of both atonement and Jubilee requires sacrifice: Christ gives up His life, and so God offers the possibility of restoration with Himself, our neighbors, our enemies, and even creation.[130]

The promised inheritance of the land, given to Israel in the Old Testament, becomes a promise of an inheritance of the Kingdom of God in the New Testament, embracing all of creation and the cosmos to all those who are in Christ (Ps. 2:8; Gal. 3:29). Romans describes the way that the whole of creation has been waiting for the

---

129   "Theology of Jubilee," *Tear Fund*, 4.
130   "Theology of Jubilee," *Tear Fund*, 5.

time when the children of God are revealed (8:19-22), waiting for the restoration of God's original plan for humanity to rule creation as God's image bearers. However, this life is not easy: Jesus's life and death show us the lengths to which the Son of God went in order to secure our liberation. We are called to likewise take up our cross (Mt. 16:24) and follow Him in obedience. This sacrifice, again, is more than generosity: it is a willingness to honor God's sovereignty and to make reparations for sin in order to end injustice and enable restoration and flourishing.[131]

United By Love

Although the influence of Josiah Royce on King's conception of the Beloved Community is contested, scholars readily concede that Royce's ideas exerted, as Rufus Burrow puts it, "at least an indirect influence on King's socio-ethical thought." The African American experience altered significantly, if not decisively, the socio-ethical trajectory of this metaphor—namely, "the Beloved Community," within the history of philosophy and theology in America. Admittedly, Royce's philosophical speculations on the Beloved Community and loyalty to loyalty itself can sometimes seem quite remote from Thurman's work with the Church for the Fellowship of All Peoples in San Francisco, or King's activist-advocacy work with the civil rights movement from Montgomery to Memphis.[132]

The influence of Royce on Thurman and King was but one of many significant factors or variables in a complex confluence of sociohistorical and philosophical influences; still, the philosophical influence or impact of Royce's teachings on Thurman and King was nonetheless nontrivial. And while the genius of Thurman or King cannot be reduced to the ideas of their predecessors, whether Royce and Du Bois, intellectual or cultural, I believe that something valuable is gained by revisiting the philosophical history as well as the pragmatic meaning of this trope from Royce to Thurman and King.[133]

---

131 "Theology of Jubilee," *Tear Fund*, 6.
132 "The Growing Edges of Beloved Community: From Royce to Thurman and King," *Transactions of the Charles S. Peirce Society* 52, no. 2 (Spring 2016): 240, accessed December 19, 2018, doi:10.2979/trancharpeirsoc.52.2.07.
133 "The Growing Edges of Beloved Community," 242.

For Royce, the Beloved Community "does not consist simply in making a transition from an individual to a social level, but in the establishment of that special community which does not breed individualism because it embodies some higher and therefore super-human form of love powerful enough to transform the individual and at the same time do away with the fatal outcome of natural social cultivation which is based on nothing higher than human talents and potentials." Royce understood in his own way that participating in a community united by love transforms the individual. This transfiguring relationship, this "mystery of loving membership in a community whose meaning seems divine," is for Royce the "specific condition" of that particular authenticity that constitutes "the graced or Beloved Community." Royce thought that religious communities allow us "to carry on, even after serious defeat and loss, and to believe that our experience of finitude will not be the last word."[134]

> *If the gospel has nothing to say to people as they confront the daily realities of life, it is a lifeless message.*

The philosophical or religious metaphor of the Beloved Community, diversely envisioned, is an informative if not also inspiring lens through which, as Thurman put it, "to perceive a harmony that transcends all diversities and in which diversity finds its richness and significance." Royce, as well as Thurman and King, was committed to building a Beloved Community, that is, a human community built on love because they were each convinced that "their help was needed." The sort of help that was needed, as they perceived sympathetically yet intelligently, was diverse, certainly; but there is a shared yet growing edge of the "provincialism" that stretches (if not strives) toward increasingly non-exclusionary loyalties. In this sense, Royce's philosophy of loyalty constitutes a socio-ethical ideal:

> Reverberating all through you, stirring you to your depths, loyalty first unifies your plan of life, and thereby gives you what nothing else can give – viz., your Self as a life lived in accordance with a

---

134   "The Growing Edges of Beloved Community," 242.

plan, your conscience as your plan interpreted for you through your ideal, your cause as your personal purpose in living.[135]

Beyond the "legal aspect of integration," which involves changes in policies and regulations, and is understood as a mechanical movement from segregation to desegregation to integration, Thurman emphasized a "second meaning of integration that has to do with the quality of human relations." In 1966, he described the dynamic meaning of integration this way:

> During the years when the Church for the Fellowship of All Peoples in San Francisco was being developed, it became increasingly clear that the mere presence of people of different ethnic or cultural backgrounds in the membership did not mean that the church itself was integrated. The coming together of people in such institutions must be rooted in natural communal association. They must be able to participate meaningfully in the various phases of their living if their relationship is to be positive and creative. Meaningful experiences of integration between people are more compelling than the fears, the inhibitions, the dogmas, or the prejudices that divide. If such unifying experiences can be multiplied over an extended time, they will be able to restructure the fabric of the social context.[136]

Thurman sought to build a Beloved Community as a living confirmation or empirical validation of what he considered to be a profound religious and ethical insight concerning the genius of the church as a religious fellowship. Thurman's *Footprints of a Dream* recounts the origins and results of his experiment in community-building, which put to the test his working hypothesis, namely, that "A way could be found to unite people of great ideological and religious diversity through experiences which were more compelling than the concepts that separated and divided."[137]

Lawrence N. Jones and Rufus Burrow, among others, have suggested that "Blacks have been searching for the Beloved Community for as long as they have been in this country."

---

135   "The Growing Edges of Beloved Community," 242.
136   "The Growing Edges of Beloved Community," 246.
137   "The Growing Edges of Beloved Community," 247.

A Theology of Liberation

According to William Banks, Black liberation theology began to take root during the time of slavery in America. At that time, most Blacks accepted the *slave brand* of Christianity on face value. White missionaries persuaded Blacks that life on earth was insignificant because obedient servants of God could expect a reward in heaven after death. The white interpretation of Christianity effectively divested the slaves of any concern that they might have had about their freedom in the present.[138]

James Cone states that as more Blacks began attending white Christian churches, restrictions in seating, communion services, and property ownership caused many Blacks to seek autonomy in their own congregations and, ultimately, separate denominations.[139] By the mid-1700s, Black slaves had begun meeting in private to worship since authentic worship with whites was impossible. There is historical evidence to conclude that the themes later developed by Black liberation theologians were present in these early slave meetings in at least a nascent form.[140]

Emmanuel McCall reminds us that it was not long before slave theology gave rise to Black activism.[141] Many important figures contributed to the cause of Black liberation throughout Black history. Among them were Nat Turner, Marcus Garvey, Howard Thurman, Martin Luther King Jr., and Albert Cleage. However, Black liberation theology was not alone among the earliest forms of liberation theology.

Christian Smith explains that liberation theology, which resembles Black liberation theology, surfaced in 1955.[142] At that time, the Latin American Episcopal Conference pushed the Second Vatican Council (1963-1965) toward a more socially-oriented stance. During the next four years, the Latin American Episcopal Conference began to explore and even support liberation theology. Cardinal Alphonso

---

138   William L. Banks, *Black Church in the US* (Chicago, IL: Moody Press, 1972), 12.

139   James H. Cone, *Black Theology and Black Power* (New York, NY: Seabury Press, 1969), 121.

140   Cone, *Black Theology and Black Power*, 121.

141   Emmanuel McCall, *Black Liberation Theology: A Politics of Freedom* (Durham, NC: Duke University Press, 1990), 352.

142   Christian Smith, *Emergence of Liberation Theology: Radical Religion and the Social Movement Theory* (Chicago, IL: University of Chicago Press, 1991), 2.

Lopez Trujillo stated that the gathering of Roman Catholic bishops officially supported a version of liberation theology.

Later, several essays were published on liberation theology in the 1970s, and one of the most famous is by the Peruvian Catholic priest, Friar Gustavo Gutierrez.[143] In his 1972 book, *A Theology of Liberation*, Gutierrez theorized a combination of Marxism and the social-Catholic teachings contributing to a socialist current in the Church.

In essence, liberation theology explores the relationship between Christian, particularly Roman Catholic, theology and political activism, particularly in areas of social justice, poverty and human rights.[144] It is this same sense of activism that would mark the awakening of Black liberation theology.

According to Pleins, the idea of being brought out of crisis is captivating for the oppressed. Pleins argues that in modern contexts of oppression, the ancient story of the God who leads slaves out of the harshness of oppression toward the Promised Land has had the power to capture political imagination.[145] Pleins states that African Americans have long been inspired by this story. Through a Latin American liberation reading, the Exodus story has functioned as a resource and guide for the Church's involvement in the task of human liberation. Pleins indicates that the persuasive appeal of the Exodus theme as a ground for liberation is also evidenced by its impact on Christian discourse in the South African context.[146]

Eric Lincoln makes the argument that prophetic preaching must be relevant to truly liberate individuals from crisis. He states that Black liberation theology as expressed in the African American community seeks to find a way to make the gospel relevant to Black people who must struggle daily under the burden of white oppression.[147] The question often posed to Black theologians is not one that is easily answered. "What, if anything, does the Christian gospel have to say to powerless

---

143   Gustavo Gutierrez, *A Theology of Liberation: History, Politics and Salvation* (New York, NY: Orbis Books, 1988), 2.

144   Gutierrez, *A Theology of Liberation*, 2.

145   J. David Pleins, *Social Visions of the Hebrew Bible* (Louisville, KY: Westminster John Knox Press, 2001), 12.

146   Pleins, *Social Visions of the Hebrew Bible,* 12.

147   Eric C. Lincoln, "The Development of Black Religion in America," *Review and Expositor* 70 (Summer 1973), 12.

Black men," to use James Cone's words, whose existence is "threatened on a daily basis by the insidious tentacles of white power?" If the gospel has nothing to say to people as they confront the daily realities of life, it is a lifeless message. If Christianity is not real to Blacks, then they will reject it.[148]

In Wilmore and Cone's work, "Black Theology: A Document History," they make the case that there were also many reasons to believe that many African Americans previously rejected Christianity.[149] The historical presence of Islam in the African American community was nurtured by a variety of forces, but one of its principal sources of strength was the sense that within many Blacks a tremendous gap existed between what took place in church on Sunday, and how church people lived during the rest of the week.[150] Many converts to Islam were Christian, but they testified to seeing little coherence between the worship of the Church, and the rough and tumble world of the streets the rest of the week.[151]

According to Lincoln, James Cone is known as the father of Black liberation theology.[152] Cone was born in Fordyce, Arkansas in 1939, and grew up in the small town of Bearsden.[153] It was there that Cone experienced the life-affirming community of the Black church alongside the soul-crushing reality of white racism. Through sermons, songs, and prayers that called on God's concern for their well-being, the Macedonia African Methodist Episcopal (AME) Church taught Cone how to deal with the contradictions of life and presented a way to create meaning in a society not of his own making.[154]

Wilmore and Cone explain that it was the voice of Malcolm X that first made Cone question his theology.[155] Malcolm X proclaimed that "Christianity was a white man's religion," and said that Blacks should adopt an understanding of God

---

148   Lincoln, "The Development of Black Religion,"12.

149   Gayraud S. Wilmore and James H. Cone, *Black Theology: A Documentary History* (New York, NY: Orbis Press, 1979), 116-117.

150   Wilmore and Cone, *Black Theology*, 116.

151   Wilmore and Cone, *Black Theology*, 116.

152   Lincoln, *"Development of Black Religion in America,"* 12.

153   Emmanuel McCall, *Black Liberation Theology: A Politics of Freedom* (Durham, NC: Duke University Press, 1990), 352

154   McCall, *Black Liberation Theology*, 352.

155   Wilmore and Cone, *Black Theology*, 116-117.

that grew out of their own history and experience. Still, it was the northern riots and Stokely Carmichael's call for "Black Power" during the Meredith March in Mississippi that led him to a crisis in faith. Cone verifies that he was within inches of leaving the Christian faith until he found it absolutely necessary to reinterpret his faith to respond to such demanding times. The Black Power and Civil Rights movements not only unveiled the crisis of the Black community, but empowered that community to envision and expand itself beyond a history of racial injustice. In this way, the Black Power and Civil Rights movements led to the onset of political, social, and financial liberation movements.[156]

Black Theology Today

Dale Andrews describes the role of Black theology as a prophetic tradition that lays claim to "Black Power" for the Black church. He states that it asserts this claim without validated self-knowledge or understanding and without the scrutiny of the Black church. Accordingly, he maps out the "chasm" that currently exists between the academy and the Black church in its cultural "beliefs, values, passions, worldview, and ways of knowing." On the one hand, he states that Black theologians charge that the Black churches have abandoned their liberation history for another form of spirituality that is inadequate for helping them overcome racial and economic oppression. On the other hand, churches charge Black theologians with advancing a political agenda for Black power at the expense of the universal gospel message of Christian love.[157]

Andrews also identifies several key dynamics that currently put the Black church and Black theologians' estranged relationship in perspective. He argues that while Black theologians must avoid the adversarial rhetoric and seek to understand Black churches are indifferent to charges of otherworldliness and social irrelevance, Black churches must not dismiss Black theologians as reductionist. Andrews's analysis suggests that there is uniformity of perspective among Black churches that makes

---

156   Wilmore and Cone, *Black Theology*, 117.
157   Mark Gawaine Harden, "Toward a Practical Black Theology and Liberation Ethic: An Alternative African-American Perspective," *Black Theology* 9, no. 1 (April 2011): 35–55, accessed January 3, 2019, doi:10.1558/bkth.v9i1.35.

developing an agenda for collective action aligned with Black theology unlikely due to the "new emphasis" on "personal salvation framed by individualism." Andrews holds that the best Black theology comes from the Black church's self-understanding. To achieve this clarity of self-understanding, it will need the objective analysis of Black theologians.[158]

Nevertheless, this religious dynamic seems inadequately explored or addressed by Black theologians. As a result, Black theology strains to remain relevant for all who claim the Black experience in the Black church. Some who feel estranged from the theological discourse of Black theologians feel this inadequacy keenly. Historically, racial identity relegated Black people to second-class status regardless of their ability to achieve greater standing in society. For many, symbolic Jim Crowism continues to demoralize and maintain the status quo in a system that divides the haves from the have-nots, leaving the have-nots to fill the role of second-class citizenship. In the meantime, individualism and the forces of integration have rendered many issues difficult to collectively address from a mutual aid perspective from within the Black church.[159]

A broad and relevant Black theology is one that is instrumental for individual empowerment in achieving equity and social justice. The question of the Black power claim is an important one to revisit, because it may direct our attention to another conclusion as to what Black theology and the Black struggle are about: namely, individual empowerment in an individualistic and oppressive society. Individualism and integration forces redefine the collective bond ideally shaped by those with shared experiences, while the forces of assimilation also function to perpetuate division and exclusion within the African American community. The lack of individual power to overcome injustice is an important issue for Black theologians to consider, and a necessary foundation for any model that seeks to build the Beloved Community.[160]

---

158   Harden, "Toward a Practical Black Theology," 38.
159   Harden, "Toward a Practical Black Theology," 41.
160   Harden, "Toward a Practical Black Theology," 42.

| CHAPTER EIGHT |

Practical Resources

In order for New Jericho Christian Church to position itself to become the Beloved Community, there needed to be radical change in how members saw themselves in relation to those around them. The church needed to reinvent itself by becoming aware of the power of scripture in solving the problems it faced.

With this goal, we sought to engage the congregation in an in-depth examination of the biblical text. From the Old and New Testaments, the lessons on Jubilee and being the Body of Christ were used. Resources in community organizing, community development, transforming communities, and becoming the Beloved Community augmented the biblical text and served as additional teaching aids and tools.

This project used pre- and post-tests, sermons and a church/community workshop to prepare the congregation and the community stakeholders for becoming the Beloved Community, all of which I have included below. The pre and post-tests determined the degree by which participants grew in their understanding of the subject matter, especially the Beloved Community. Sermons were used to allow the congregation and guests to hear what the word of God says about caring for the widow and orphan, canceling debts, treating one another as brothers and sisters in Christ, and the significance of being the Body of Christ. The church/community workshop was designed to allow for a free flow of information exchange. This was also a time when real needs were articulated, and the extent, if any, we could expect support from city, county and state officials toward a model of the Beloved Community.

WHY USE A QUESTIONNAIRE?

The pre-test questionnaire examined the level of knowledge participants had about their community, community organizing, transforming communities, and the Beloved Community before they were exposed to the project, as well as any of the learning they gleaned from the various presentations and discussions. This helped us hear more broadly from congregation members over a period of time.

At the end of the project, when all testing and learning had been completed, a post-test was administered using the same questions as the pre-test. The results of the pre-test were then compared to the results from the post-test to determine the overall level of learning of each participant. Closer examinations also occurred with questions that had the greatest deviation, to assess the validity of probing deeper into those areas for greater clarification and explanation.

What we saw was that the results from the pre- and post-test questionnaires indicated an increase in knowledge toward the importance and value of what it meant to be a Beloved Community. It also indicated a desire on the part of the participants to move toward transforming their existing community into a Beloved Community.

Pre- and Post-test Questions

Rate the following responses either true or false based on your understanding of your context of ministry.

COMMUNITY AWARENESS QUESTIONS	PRE-TEST	POST-TEST	DEVIATION
I am satisfied with the services I receive from my community			
Community organizations care about those of us who find it difficult to find jobs and provide for ourselves and our families			
There are adequate shelters in my community			
I feel safe alone at night in my community			
Police have a low opinion of homeless and persons relegated to live in shelters			
My church is actively involved in providing for the needs of the have not's in this community			
My pastor encourages community outreach			
I am aware of what a Beloved Community is			
My community would benefit from becoming a Beloved Community			
I would work to make my community a Beloved Community			

WHY A SERMON SERIES?

The sermon series was based on two sermons, one from the Old and New Testaments. The sermons were based on the biblical foundations discussed earlier in Chapter Five, and centered on uncovering the hermeneutical meaning for practical application in the project context.

Leviticus 25

The first sermon from the Old Testament book of Leviticus 25 was entitled "When Social Concern Becomes a True Test of Faith." The thesis of this text was based on the faith of the Israelites to follow the instructions given to Moses by God. In essence, the entire 25th chapter can be divided into seven movements, with each movement systematically building to a full understanding of what God intends for His people. The seven movements are as follows:

- God desires his people to operate out of rest. The result of rest is an increase in yield.

- The sabbatical year stands for liberation; God requires the Israelites to work out liberation in principle. In the last of seven sabbatical years, liberation will fully manifest itself in completion.

- Once liberation occurs, there must be a time of restoration.

- Rest plus liberation plus restoration equals abundance. In the year of Jubilee, God, not the land, will provide for all we need.

- Nothing we have, we have forever; it all belongs to God and at an appointed time, God will redeem it.

- If persons are too poor to settle their debts, take care of them and do not leave them unable to do anything about it.

- The life of the land is preserved in righteousness, and the life of humanity is also preserved in righteousness.

The year of Jubilee is born out of the principle of sabbath or rest. While the text is primarily concerned with the land, it also applies to human life. Just as we are to allow the land to rest in order to gain a greater harvest, so it is with humanity: when we treat one another with decency and respect and set aside time for forgiveness, God provides for us in the same way he provides for the land. The Beloved Community can only take place when people take a step back and begin to help and empower others to have a greater quality of life.

Questions from Leviticus 25

On a scale of 1-5, rate the following statements as they apply to your context of ministry. These questions pertain to your understanding of the biblical text in relation to the command of God to be involved in social justice ministries as a way of building up the Kingdom of God.

1=highly disagree   2=disagree   3=neutral   4=agree   5=highly agree

I did not fully understand the meaning of the text before the lesson	
The lesson changed my understanding of the text	
I was convicted by the lesson that was taught	
The lesson empowered me to action	
The lesson made me feel ashamed of my actions as a Christian	
The lesson created a need to develop the Beloved Community	
More members of the church need to have this lesson	
The lesson needs to be taught again for better clarity	
After the lesson, I am willing to assist in creating the Beloved Community	

1 Corinthians 12

The second sermon comes from the New Testament book of 1 Corinthians 12, entitled "The Body or Body Parts," and was designed to have members understand the intricacies of the human body and its ability to function when all parts function as they are intended. This sermon had four basic movements:

- How we think of the body

- How we think of ourselves

- How we think of others

- Unity in diversity.

Ultimately, this sermon can be summed up with these lyrics from the song, "I Need You to Survive."

> I need you; you need me, we are all a part of God's body. Stand with me, agree with me, we are all a part of God's body. It is his will, that every need be supplied. You are important to me; I need you to survive. I pray for you; you pray for me. I love you; I need you to survive. I will not harm you with words from my mouth. I love you; I need you to survive. It is his will, that every need be supplied. You are important to me; I need you to survive.[161]

Questions from 1 Corinthians 12

On a scale of 1-5, rate the following statements as they apply to your context of ministry. These questions pertain to your understanding of the biblical text in relation to the command of God to be involved in social justice ministries as a way of building up the Kingdom of God.

---

161   Hezekiah Walker, "I Need You To Survive," accessed May 4, 2019, https://www.lyrics.com/lyric/6799583/Hezekiah+Walker/I+Need+You+To+Survive

1=highly disagree   2=disagree   3=neutral   4=agree   5=highly agree

I did not fully understand the meaning of the text before the lesson	
The lesson changed my understanding of the text	
I was convicted by the lesson that was taught	
The lesson empowered me to action	
The lesson made me feel ashamed of my actions as a Christian	
The lesson created a need to create the body of Christ in my church	
More members of the church need to have this lesson	
The lesson needs to be taught again for better clarity	
After the lesson, I am willing to assist in creating the body of Christ at my church	

WHY A CHURCH AND COMMUNITY WORKSHOP?

The church and community workshop was designed to foster relationships with the residents of the community in such a way that genuine partnerships and relationships could occur. Law enforcement, social services, economic development specialists, church leaders, the homeless and other concerned citizens were all invited to participate in this critical event in the life of the church.

Questions From the Workshop

What do you believe is your responsibility in meeting the needs of those less fortunate than you?

_____

_____

_____

What is your understanding of the Beloved Community?

_____

_____

_____

How does this understanding impact your role in the life of the Church?

_____

_____

_____

Identify how you will increase your participation in the outreach ministry of the church.

_____

_____

_____

| CHAPTER NINE |

What Does It Take to Succeed?

As we were determining the most effective models of implementing the Beloved Community in church contexts, a tremendous amount of time and effort went into the design and development of the research methods mentioned in the previous chapter. Without conducting the appropriate level of research, support for the various agencies and social service institutions would have not been possible, and accurate decisions could not have been made. The resources above were also created to take into consideration various educational levels, reading comprehension levels, and abilities.

As I look back on my years building the Beloved Community here at New Jericho Church, having a heart for the least of these was another critical factor in our success. Luckily, we had positive support and enthusiasm for what was being proposed and people were truly interested in assisting in making a difference for the sake of the whole community. The members of the church who volunteered to participate were true angels. With the wealth of work that needed to be done in various areas and at various times, this work would have been next to impossible to do without their input and support.

HOW TO USE THESE RESOURCES

If you are interested in implementing these same methods of research and evaluation in your own church, a few words of encouragement and advice:

Pre- and Post-tests: We used the above pre- and post-tests to gauge the level of knowledge gained throughout the process. By assessing both knowledge prior to exposure and knowledge gained after learning, we could gather critical information in considering the level of engagement that should be taken in the future. I encourage you to look at these tools as a way to invite your church body into a more active reflection on these topics.

Sermons: Sermons are the bedrock of the church and the gospel ministry, the most effective way to share the word of God. Using sermons that illuminate the biblical text and shed light on the context is the most effective way to modify current behavior, culture and systems. By mixing sermons with an opportunity for engagement and response, you invite the entire congregation to begin paying attention to biblical themes and the ways they intersect with your specific community.

Workshops: Finally, workshops allow large numbers of people who are stakeholders in the community to gather in one place for the purpose of providing assistance for the community residents, and aiding in a greater quality of life for all. When the community comes together with the expressed purpose of solving a common problem, it increases the sense of hope and possibility.

After completing these phases at New Jericho Christian Church, we found that the church body was much better prepared to implement the vision of the Beloved Community. Below are a few case studies as examples of what kind of transformation is possible:

Case Study #1: Community Outreach

As a church body, we re-examined our community outreach and determined what would most evidence the love of Christ in our neighborhood. To begin, we began offering free food and clothing events in our parking lot that blew people away. Actually, first we had to convince people that the food was free and that the clothing was not a yard sale! Because our goal was that it would not look like charity, from the outside it looked like a church fundraiser or another community function - expensive barbecue, greens, the kind of meal you might buy for thirty dollars. But if you engaged us, you discovered it was about love for the community: a free hot meal with some dignity and pride. The same went for the clothing - we had a limited amount to give away, but what we did give were items that people would have wanted to buy. This made a huge impact in a community that has often received the leftovers from others. Pretty soon people started inviting their friends! They also knew that if they were ever interested in church, we were right here, and this blend of generosity without strings attached has been incredibly powerful.

Case Study #2: Child Development Center

Through our research, we discovered that our community included a lot of children that were not being watched or cared for, because community programs were not funded for latchkey children or after-school care. Children were walking home or remaining on the school campus unsupervised, basically raising themselves for up to eight to ten hours a day. They were faced with molestation, violence, and bullying - all in the absence of a parent or adult supervisor.

We saw that as part of the Beloved Community, the church could create after-school programs and tutoring to meet the needs of the child between the hours of 2:30 and 6 pm, just three and a half hours a day. In the local community, there was no other safe place during that time. If we gave kids a safe space to land, we reasoned, we could not only provide activities, but could address mental health issues through volunteers, such as graduate-level students working on their counseling or social work degree.

Volunteers like this did step forward, and thanks to their efforts, children could now receive free counseling. Next, we began thinking about mentors as well. Some of the local fraternities and Big Sister/Big Brother programs, as well as other great mentors from our church, began meeting with students and sometimes even tutoring them in subjects in which they struggled. We began to identify people at church - engineers and schoolteachers, for example - who could volunteer a little time. From there, we started looking at issues like teen pregnancy, the situation of former foster youth, formerly incarcerated youth, etc. We asked ourselves: what if we offered some parenting classes, or classes on peer pressure or anger management or bullying? How could we address the violence in this community and establish a safe zone? In this way, we found ourselves creating programs that the community needed.

Case Study #3: Family Support

We wanted to create a safe space, a place that people felt comfortable stepping in and would not feel "churchy." So we asked each other, "Okay, what about the individual who is homeless? How do we help the child of that parent who's living in their car?" The church became a place to have safe overnight parking. Soon, kids were sleeping in the safe parking lot in their car, at the church where they're now going to a safe place after school. What about a meal while they are there, or a snack? So we began providing more meal services. We also connected them with social services that have housing assistance vouchers, hotel vouchers, and services that would help them find permanent housing. After learning that most families become homeless after missing just one single paycheck, we provided gas vouchers and gift cards, and assisted with utility bills so families did not have to choose between paying the electricity bill and paying rent. We have seen some low-level crime taper off, because people no longer have to commit crimes out of financial pressures, which means parents are no longer separated from their children.

As each of these three initiatives was underway, we started saying to ourselves, "Okay, now we're addressing what the community really needs." We were offering social services that not only provided a service but were turning a behavior around. We saw people finding wholeness and healing. Incredibly, all this has happened, even when we have not even mentioned anything from the Bible to them yet! To me, this is what it means to be a Christian and provide the services that people need, sharing the love of Christ in such a tangible way.

In everything we do, we want people to come away with dignity and pride, to know they are in a safe zone and feel they can talk and be very open with us. We would not be able to do this if we had not established this openness to the community and been able to assess and identify needs. It is this kind of proximity, creativity, and openness that determines the Beloved Community.

CONCLUSION

The Beloved Community is a global vision in which all people can share in the wealth of the earth. In the Beloved Community, poverty, hunger, and homelessness will not be tolerated because international standards of human decency will not allow it. Racism and all forms of discrimination, bigotry, and prejudice will be replaced by an all-inclusive spirit of sisterhood and brotherhood.[162]

MARTIN LUTHER KING JR.

Slowly, our community at New Jericho Christian Church is starting to look more like the Beloved Community that Martin Luther King Jr. described above. As we have traveled this journey, our goal has been to deliver a service to individuals in the local community who would normally pass the church by. We have seen that as they realize there are no strings attached, people begin to feel more comfortable interacting with us. After being at a place where they receive help without any proselytizing, they want to be a part of the church community that offers that service. In this way, the Beloved Community provides a critical understanding of what it means to live as the Body of Christ while establishing the Kingdom of God in our lifetime.

I can share from experience that this mindset has completely changed our community as we work and come together with this goal. We have developed solutions to address the problems we identified together; we have recruited people to provide services accordingly; and we have delivered the services free of charge. And those who received the services have returned to us. They have gained a much higher respect of the Church and of Christians. They take more pride in themselves and

---

162 "The Beloved Community: Martin Luther King Jr.'s Prescription for a Healthy Society," December 6, 2017, *Huff Post*, accessed September 22, 2018, https://www.huffingtonpost. com/ jeffrey-ritterman/the-beloved-community-dr-_b_4583249.html.

come out of the shell where they hid their brokenness. They connect with their community and with the church, and appreciate the services they receive.

When I look at this work today, I remember all the years I was growing up hungry at church, unable to eat because we did not have the money to pay for it. It means so much to me that children who went through what I have gone through can come to the church in our neighborhood and get a good meal free of charge. Now, we can address their needs like the church could have addressed my mother's all that time ago. We have the chance to be the community these children and families need.

Through the past forty-five years, I have learned that God never wastes the experiences of our past. Although I never want children to go through what I went through, I am confident that God miraculously preserved my life all those years ago in order to direct me to this work today. I look back on my life and see God's hand of faithfulness, as he used those experiences to allow me to offer wisdom and compassion to others who are in the same situations.

Despite the social ills we are experiencing all around us, our work at New Jericho Christian Church is living proof that the Beloved Community is a path forward toward a more civil society, where a sense of equality and justice prevails. After all, the Beloved Community's core mission is to reveal and to heal issues—to honestly confront them and to compassionately make corrections as they unfold. For this to happen, the church must be transformed from a corporate mindset to becoming disciples of Christ who follow a biblical model for building the Kingdom. As Lockard reminds us, the Beloved Community is about being truly dedicated to walking your talk—to being in full alignment with spiritual principles.[163] When we focus on trust, dignity, and strength-based community assessment, what will emerge is a vision for not only the needs of our particular community, but the gifts it has to offer.

As you can see from the case studies in Chapter Nine, the opportunity is great - even when the need appears still greater. The more we begin to creatively address the needs of our community, the more interrelated we understand them to be. This is both the challenge and the great blessing of where we find ourselves today.

---

163   Jim Lockard, *Creating the Beloved Community: A Handbook for Spiritual Leadership* (n.p. Jim Lockard, 2017), 1.

Because of the high percentage of people in our community living below the poverty line, no one church can solve these problems alone. We need each other. Therefore, our next goal is to train partner churches to join us, believing that there is no competition in the Kingdom - the more we spread, the more like the Beloved Community we will become.

We serve a God who cares about the whole human being, and the whole community. As people of faith, we are called in turn to care for the whole human being and the whole community. If, after reading this book, you have begun to catch a vision of what this community could look like, I encourage you that it is possible anywhere, anytime - not just for a select few churches that do everything right. In every context, we are seeking a community that addresses the whole person - a place of integrated worship, social services, youth programs, and civic engagement initiatives. We are seeking a place where the church can be the Church, even without words.

Jubilee theology does not have to stay in the pulpit. The Body of Christ does not have to stay within the church doors. In fact, The Great Commission becomes the impetus for building God's Kingdom on earth. A Beloved Community is ultimately one where everyone is a follower of Jesus Christ and lives out the commands of God. While there is more work to be done, and more people to receive the love of God that is found in Christ Jesus, the ground is pregnant with possibility: the Beloved Community can emerge as God intended. We can walk forward in faith, knowing it is the will of God for His people.

ABOUT THE AUTHOR

DR. WENDELL J. DAVIS, SR.

Dr. Wendell J. Davis, Sr., MATS, DMIN, Ph.D., CDAC, CFC, attended public school in Los Angeles and graduated from John C. Fremont High School in 1985. He attended Los Angeles Mission College and earned a BA in Christian Education in 1996, and an MA in Christian Counseling and Psychology from Southwestern Bible College and Seminary in Jennings, Louisiana, in 1999. He earned his Ph.D. in Christian Counseling at Louisiana Baptist University in 2003, was a graduate of Faith Seminary in Tacoma, Washington with a DMIN in Strategic Leadership in 2011, and received a DMIN in Community Development at Payne Theological Seminary in 2021 in Wilberforce, OH - the oldest Black Seminary in America.

Dr. Davis Is the former two-term President of Alumni at USC Cecil Murray Center Dornside School and a former Board Member. Dr. Davis founded and organized New Jericho Christian Church in 2007, in Compton, California. Dr. Davis has 28 years of pastoral experience and is the CEO of Trinity In His House Foundation #1, Inc., a nonprofit faith-based agency providing transitional housing for drug and alcohol recovery, child care services, and counseling education, which he organized 26 years ago. He formerly served as Vice President of Community and Civic Engagement at the Historical Baptist Minister Conference of LA. The author of *Lost But Not Hopeless* and the accompanying workbook, *Healing A Wounded Leader*, and *Marriage & Family Therapies*, Dr. Davis is the former Supervisor of Substance Abuse Programs at California Correctional facilities, and a certified instructor for the National Baptist Convention USA. He also served as Executive Secretary and Vice Moderator of the LADA of the WBSC, the eldest African American Baptist Convention in California, and 2nd Vice Moderator of Providence Baptist Associations of the California State Baptist Convention. Dr. Davis currently serves as

Presiding Bishop of Macedonia International Christian Fellowship, where he gives leadership to 21 churches across the United States and one in Trinidad and Tabago.

Dr. Davis is married to the lovely Trevina Davis, his wife of 37 years. They have two beautiful children, Wendell Jr., 37, and Wenikka, 34; two granddaughters, Lyric, 10, and Laylah, 5; and one grandson, Legend Deuce Elcan Davis, 1.5 years old. Dr. Davis loves serving God and His people.

BIBLIOGRAPHY

Ammerman, Nancy. *Congregation and Community*. New Brunswick, NJ: Rutgers University Press, 1997.

Banks, William L. *Black Church in the US*. Chicago, IL: Moody Press, 1972.

Barna, George. *Leaders On Leadership: Wisdom, Advice, and Encouragement On the Art of Leading God's People*. The Leading Edge Series. Grand Rapids, MI: Baker Books, 2014.

_____. *The Habits of Highly Effective Churches: Being Strategic in Your God-Given Ministry*. Ventura, CA: Regal Books, 1999.

Barnes, Rebecca, Lindy Lowry. "Special Report: The American Church in Crisis." Outreach Magazine, May/June 2006. (Accessed June 2011). http://www. christianity today.com/outreach/articles/americanchurchcrhsis.html.

Black Theology, Project. "Message to the Black Church and community." *The Journal Of Religious Thought* 34, no. 2 (September 1977): 24, *ATLA Religion Database with ATLASerials*, EBSCO*host* (Accessed February 10, 2017).

Blackaby, Henry T. and Richard Blackaby. *Spiritual Leadership: Moving People On to God's Agenda*. Rev. ed. Nashville, TN: B & H Publishing Group, 2011.

Blanchard, Kenneth H., and Phil Hodges. *Lead like Jesus: Lessons from the Greatest Leadership Role Model of All Times*. Nashville, TN: W Pub. Group, 2005.

Bobo, Kimberley A. 1995. "Church Involvement in Community Organizations," *Review & Expositor* 92 (1): 31–38. Accessed October 18, 2018,http://proxy.payne.edu: 2061/login. aspx?direct= true&db=rfh&AN=ATLA0000893668&site=eh ost-live.

Boers, Arthur P. *Servants and Fools: A Biblical Theology of Leadership*. Nashville, TN: Abingdon Press, 2015.

Bradley, Anthony B. *Liberating Black Theology: The Bible and the Black Experience in America*. Wheaton, IL: Crossway Books, 2010.

Breen, Mike. *Building a Discipling Culture.* 2nd ed. Pawley's Island, SC: 3DM Publishing, 2014.

Bright, Bill. *Handbook for Christian Maturity: Bible Study, Ten Basic Steps Toward Christian Maturity.* Peachtree City, GA: New Life Pub., 2002.

Briner, Bob, and Ray Pritchard. *Leadership Lessons of Jesus: A Timeless Model for Today's Leaders.* Nashville, TN: B & H Publishing Group, 2008.

Brown, Michael Jacoby. *Building Powerful Community Organizations.* Arlington, MA: Long Haul Press, 2006.

Brueggemann, Walter. 1999. "The City in Biblical Perspective: Failed and Possible." *Word & World* 19, 236-250, *Old Testament Abstracts*, EBSCO*host.* (Accessed July 9, 2016).

Celek, Tim and Dieter Zander. *Inside The Soul Of A New Generation.* Grand Rapids, MI: Zondervan Publishing House.

Charleston Regional Development Alliance. "Population." Accessed April 11, 2013. www.crda.org/business /market_profile.nd.

Christensen, Michael J. and Carl E. Savage. *Equipping the Saints: Mobilizing Laity for Ministry.* Nashville, TN: Abingdon Press, 2000.

Chinula, Donald M. *Building King's Beloved Community: Foundations for Pastoral Care and Counseling with the Oppressed.* Eugene, OR: Pilgrim Press, 1997.

Cone, James H. *Black Theology and Black Power.* New York, NY: Seabury Press, 1969.

_____. *A Black Theology of Liberation,* 40th ed. Maryknoll, New York: Orbis Books, 2010. Kindle Edition.

_____. *Risks of Faith: The Emergence of a Black Theology of Liberation.* Boston, MA: Beacon Press, 2010.

Cruickshank, Jessie. "A Quick Educational History of Discipleship." Accessed October 10, 2018. https://www.100movements.com/ articles/a-quick-educational-history-on-discipleship.

Dockery, David S. ed., *Holman Bible Handbook.* Nashville, TN: Holman Bible Publishers, 1992.

Dodson, Jonathan K. *Gospel-Centered Discipleship.* Wheaton, IL: Crossway, 2012.

Dungy, Tony, and Nathan Whitaker. *The Mentor Leader*. Carol Stream, IL: Tyndale House Publishers, 2010.

Dyck, David. "Why Not Just Live Together?: Some Reflections on Covenant Community." *Direction 30*, no. 2 (Fall 2001): 211–16. Accessed October 18, 2018, http://proxy. payne.edu:2061/login.aspx?direct =true&db=rfh&AN=ATLA 000138 0042 &site=ehost-live.

Earley, Dave and Rod Dempsey. *Disciple Making Is . . .: How to Live the Great Commission with Passion and Confidence*. Nashville, TN: B&H Publishing Group, 2013.

Endres, John C. S. J. s.v. "Book of Jubilees." ed. David Noel Freedman, Allen C. Myers, and Astrid B. Beck, *Eerdmans Dictionary of the Bible*. Grand Rapids, MI: W.B. Eerdmans, 2000.

Frank, Thomas Edward. *The Soul of the Congregation: An Invitation to Congregational Reflection*. Nashville: Abingdon Press, 2000.

Franklin, Robert Michael. *Crisis in the Village: Restoring Hope in African American Communities*. Minneapolis, MN: Fortress Press, 2007.

Frazier, F. Franklin. *The Negro Church in America*. Liverpool, UK: Liverpool University, 1964.

Geiger, Eric, Michael Kelley, and Philip Nation. *Transformational Discipleship: How People Really Grow*. Nashville, TN: B&H Books, 2012.

Guin, Jim. "The New Perspective: A Theology of Community." *One In Jesus*, Accessed February 3, 2017, http://oneinjesus.info/2007/11/ the-new-perspective-the-theology-of-community/.

Gutierrez, Gustavo. *A Theology of Liberation: History, Politics and Salvation*. New York, NY: Orbis Books, 1988.

Hamilton, Adam. *Leading Beyond the Walls: Developing Congregations with a Heart for the Unchurched*. Nashville, TN: Abingdon Press, 2002.

Hammett, Edward H. *Spiritual Leadership in a Secular Age: Building Bridges Instead of Barriers*. St. Louis, MO: Lake Hickory Resources, 2005.

Helmick, Raymond G. and Rodney Lawrence Petersen, eds. *Forgiveness and Reconciliation: Religion, Public Policy and Conflict Transformation*. Philadelphia, PA: Templeton Foundation Press, 2002.

Harden, Mark Gawaine. "Toward a Practical Black Theology and Liberation Ethic: An Alternative African-American Perspective." *Black Theology* 9, no. 1 (April 2011): 35–55, Accessed January 3, 2019. doi:10.1558/bkth.v9i1.35

Hunt, Tony "10 Ways to Build the Beloved Community." *Lewis Center For Church Leadership: Leading Ideas.* January 11, 2017. Accessed January 2, 2019, https: // www.church leadership .com/leading-ideas/ten-ways-build-beloved-community/.

Hunter, George G. *The Apostolic Congregation: Church Growth Reconceived for a New Generation.* Nashville, TN: Abingdon Press, 2009.

_____. *To Spread the Power: Church Growth in the Wesleyan Spirit.* Nashville, TN: Abingdon Press, 1987.

Hunter, George G. III. *Radical Outreach.* Nashville, TN: Abingdon Press, 2003.

Hybels, Bill. *Courageous Leadership.* Grand Rapids, MI: Zondervan, 2012.

Jeanrond, Werner G. *Call and Response: The Challenge of Christian Life.* New York, NY: Continuum Publishers, 1995.

Johnson, Ronnie, Steve Crawley. *Following the Model of Christ by Making Disciples.* Conway, AZ: DiscipleGuide Church Resources, 2012. Kindle Edition.

Jones, Lawrence Neale. *African Americans and the Christian Churches: 1619-1860.* Cleveland, OH: Pilgrim Press, 2007.

Jones, Major J. *Black Awareness: A Theology of Hope.* Nashville, TN: Abingdon Press, 1971.

Jha, Sandhya Rani. *Transforming Communities: How People Like You Are Healing Their Neighborhoods.* Atlanta, GA: Challis Press, 2017.

Jones, Lawrence N. 1981. "Black Christians in Antebellum America: In Quest of the Beloved Community." *The Journal of Religious Thought* 38 (1): 12–19. Accessed October 19, 2018, http:// proxy.payne.edu:2061/login.aspx?direct=true&db=rfh& AN=ATLA0000786280&site=ehost-live.

Kahn, Si. *Creative Community Organizing: A Guide for Rabble Rousers, Activists, & Quiet Lovers of Justice.* San Francisco, CA: Bernett-Koehler Publishers, Inc. 2010. Knauth Robin J. DeWitt, s.v. "Year of Jubilee." ed. David Noel Freedman, Allen C. Myers, and Astrid B. Beck, *Eerdmans Dictionary of the Bible.* Grand Rapids, MI: W.B. Eerdmans, 2000.

Lincoln, Eric C. "The Development of Black Religion in America." *Review and Expositor* 70. Summer 1973.

Linthicum, Robert C. *Transforming Power: Biblical Strategies for Making a Difference in Your Community*. Downers Grove, IL: InterVarsity Press, 2003.

Mahn, Jason A, and Grace Koleczek. 2014. "What intentional Christian communities can teach the church." *Word & World* 34, no. 2: 178-187. Accessed February 23, 2017. *ATLA Religion Database with ATLASerials*, EBSCOhost.

Marsh, Charles. *The Beloved Community: How Faith Shapes Social Justice from the Civil Rights Movement to Today*. New York, NY: Basic Books, 2005.

Maxwell, John C. *Developing the Leader Within You*. Nashville, TN: Nelson Business, 1993.

McCall, Emmanuel. *Black Liberation Theology: A Politics of Freedom*. Durham, NC: Duke University Press, 1990.

McIntosh, Gary. *One Church, Four Generations: Understanding and Reaching All Ages In Your Church*. Grand Rapids, MI: Baker Books, 2002

McNeal, Reggie. *Practicing Greatness: 7 Disciplines of Extraordinary Spiritual Leaders*. San Francisco, CA: Jossey-Bass, 2006.

Messer, Donald E. *Contemporary Images of Christian Ministry*. Nashville, TN: Abingdon Press, 1989.

Naylor, Mark. "The Difference between Missions and Outreach." *Cross Cultural Impact for the 21st Century*. December 1, 2008, accessed October 17, 2018. http://ipact. nbseminary.com/the-difference-between-missions-and-outreach/.

Nelson, Alan and Gene Appel. *How to Change Your Church (Without Killing It)*. Nashville, TN: Zondervan Publishing, 2000.

New Perspectives on Evangelism: Insights from Biblical Theology, Accessed March 2016. http://www. thepaulpage.com/new-perspectives-on-evangelism-insights-from-biblical-theology/.

Pate, Steve A. and C. Gene. Wilkes. *Evangelism Where You Live: Engaging Your Community*. St. Louis, MO: Chalice Press, 2008.

Peck, M. Scott. *The Different Drum: Community Making and Peace.* Accessed February 3, 2017, http://www.entcom.eu/wp-content/uploads/2015/10/Entcom-WS-Report-Annex2.pdf.

Perkins, John. *Restoring At-risk Communities: Doing It Together and Doing It Right.* Grand Rapids, MI: Baker Book House, 1995.

Petersen, Jim. *Living Proof.* Colorado Springs, CO: NavPress, 1989.

Petty, Krista "Connecting Your Church to Your Community." Externally Focused Network, accessed February 13, 2017, http://www.faithformation2020.net / uploads/5/1/6/4/5164069/ five_steps_ to_ an_externally_focused_church.pdf.

Pleins, J. David. *Social Visions of the Hebrew Bible.* Louisville, KY: Westminster John Knox Press, 2001.

Powe, F Douglas. *New Wine, New Wineskins: How African American Congregations Can Reach New Generations.* Nashville, TN: Abingdon Press, 2012

Priest, Doug. "Seek the Shalom of the City." *New Urban World.* Accessed July 7, 2016, http://newurbanworld.org/seek-the-shalom-of-the-city/.

Putman, Jim. *Real-Life Discipleship: Building Churches That Make Disciples.* Colorado Springs, CO: NavPress, 2010.

Rainer, Thom. *Breakout Churches.* Grand Rapids, MI: Zondervan Publishing, 2005.

_____. *Autopsy of a Deceased Church: 12 Ways to Keep Yours Alive.* Nashville, Tennessee: B & H Publishing Group, 2014.

_____. *The Unchurched Next Door: Understanding Faith Stages as Keys to Sharing Your Faith.* Grand Rapids, MI: Zondervan, 2008.

Rainer, Thom S., and Eric Geiger. *Simple Church: Returning to God's Process for Making Disciples.* Nashville, TN: Broadman Press, 2006.

Rankin, Nancy Burgin, and Beverly Bowyer Coppley. *Checking Vital Signs: Assessing Your Local Church Potential.* Graham, NC: Plowpoint Press, 2007.

Raschke. Carl A. 2014. "The allure of decadent thinking: religious studies and the challenge of post-modernism." *Journal Of The American Academy Of Religion* 82, no. 2: 564-566. Accessed July 31, 2016*ATLA Religion Database with ATLASerials*, EBSCO*host*.

Reagan. Debra A. 2013. "Reclaiming the body for faith." *Interpretation* 67, no. 1: 42-57. Accessed July 12, 2016, *ATLA Religion Database with ATLASerials*, EBSCO*host*.

Ritterman, Jeff. "Building the Beloved Community: Jesus, Josiah Royce, and Martin Luther King Jr.'s Prescription for a Healthy Society." Global Catholic Climate Movement, September 10, 2017, accessed January 3, 2019, https://catholicclimate movement.global/building-the-beloved-community-martin-luther-king-jr-s-prescription-for-a-healthy-society/.

Scazzero, Peter, and Warren Bird. *The Emotionally Healthy Church: A Strategy for Discipleship That Actually Changes Lives*. Grand Rapids, MI: Zondervan, 2003. Schnase, Robert C. *Five Practices of Fruitful Congregations*. Nashville, TN: Abingdon Press, 2007.

Shelley, Marshall. *Growing Your Church Through Evangelism and Outreach*. Eugene, OR: Wipf and Stock Publishers, 1999.

Smith, Christian. *Emergence of Liberation Theology: Radical Religion and the Social Movement Theory*. Chicago, IL: University of Chicago Press, 1991.

Smith, Kenneth L. and Ira G. Zepp, Jr. "Martin Luther King's Vision of the Beloved Community. *Religion on-line*. Accessed May 5, 2017, http://www.religion-online. org/ show article .asp?title=1603.

Southerland, Dan. *Transitioning: Leading Your Church through Change*. Grand Rapids, MI: Zondervan Publishers, 2000.

Statistics and Reasons for Church Decline, Accessed March 16, 2017. http://www.intothy word .org/articlesview.asp?articleid=3.

Stowell, Joseph M. *Redefining Leadership: Character-Driven Habits of Effective Leaders*. Grand Rapids, MI: Zondervan, 2014.

_____. *Shepherding the Church: Effective Spiritual Leadership in a Changing Culture*. Chicago, IL: Moody Press, 1997.

Swanson, Roger K. and Shirley F. Clement. *The Faith-sharing Congregation: Developing a Strategy for the Congregation as Evangelist*. Nashville, TN: Discipleship Resources, 1997.

"The Distinction Between Discipleship and Disciple Making." *Facts & Trends*. September 11, 2014. Accessed October 17, 2018. https://factsandtrends.net/2014/09/11/the-distinction-between-discipleship-disciple-making-a-qa-with-dann-spader/.

"The Growing Edges of Beloved Community: From Royce to Thurman and King."
    Transactions of the Charles S. Peirce Society 52. no. 2 (Spring 2016): 240. Accessed
    December 19, 2018. doi:10.2979/trancharpeirsoc.52.2.07.

"Theology of Jubilee." *Tear Fund*. Accessed December 18, 2018.
    https://www.tear fund.org/~/media/files/wewontstop/theologyofjubilee.

Tkach, Joseph. "Working Together for the Gospel." *Grace Communion International*.
    Accessed March 13, 2017. https://www.gci.org/church/ministry/working.
    Trussell, Jacqueline. "The Theology of Martin Luther King, Jr."
    BlackandChristian.com, Accessed May 5, 2017.
    http://blackandchristian.com/articles/academy/trussell-01-02.shtml.

Watson, Merritt. 1992, "Reflections on church and ministry in a postmodern era."
    Lexington Theological Quarterly 27, no. 3: 73-79. Accessed July 31, 2016. *ATLA
    Religion Database with ATLASerials*, EBSCOhost.

Wiersbe Warren W. *Be Decisive*, "Be" Commentary Series. Wheaton, IL: Victor Books,
    1996.

Welch, Skot and Rick Wilson. *Plantation Jesus: Race, Faith, and a New Way Forward*
    Harrison, VA: Harrison Press, 2018.

Wilmore, Gayraud S. and James H. Cone, *Black Theology: A Documentary History*. New
    York, NY: Orbis Press, 1979.

Wiersbe, Warren W. *Be Holy*. "Be" Commentary Series. Wheaton, IL: Victor Books, 1996.

Wright, Christopher J. H. *The Mission of God: Unlocking the Bible's Grand Narrative*.
    Downers Grove: IL Intervarsity Press, 2006.

_____. *The Mission of God's People: A Biblical Theology of the Church's Mission* Grand
    Rapids, MI: Zondervan Publishing, 2010.

_____. "Theology of Jubilee: Biblical, Social and Ethical Perspectives." Evangelical
    Review of Theology 41 (1): 6–18. Accessed December 18, 2018. http://search.
    ebscohost.com.wilberforcepayne.idm.oclc.org/login.aspx?direct=true&d b=rfh
    &AN =ATLA. n4105437&site=ehost-live.

Zscheile, Dwight J. 2017. "Who is my neighbor?: the church's vocation in an era of shifting
    community." *Word & World* 37, no. 1: 27-36, *ATLA Religion Database with
    ATLASerials*.EBSCOhost (Accessed February 24, 2017).